HARRY GILONIS is a poet, editor, publisher, and critic writing on art, poetry, and music. His books of poetry include *Reliefs* (1988), *Pibroch* (1996), *Reading Hölderlin on Orkney* (1997), *walk the line* (2000), *eye-blink* (2010), and *For British Workers* (2017), as well as collaborations with both poets – such as *from far away* (with Tony Baker, 1998) – and visual artists, such as *Forty Fungi* (with Erica Van Horn, 1994), *Axioms* (with David Connearn, 1995), and *The Leiermann* (with David Rees, after Schubert, 1998).

Rough Breathing

selected poems

Harry Gilonis

CARCANET PRESS   MMXVIII

First published in Great Britain in 2018

by

Carcanet Press Limited
Alliance House, 30 Cross Street
Manchester M2 7AQ

A CIP catalogue record for this book is available from
the British Library, ISBN 9781784103729.

The publisher acknowledges financial assistance
from Arts Council England.

Contents

That is, the unwritten (but sounded) *H* at the beginning of some Greek words beginning with a vowel. Formerly marked with a symbol that looked like half an H (my initial initial), it's the sound at the start of my given name. Over time it simplified down to the form above. Later grammarians called it the *spiritus asper*, every bit as much 'rough spirit' as 'rough breathing'. It is also called, in a nice mix of tonalities, an 'aspiration'.

Roland Barthes, speaking of the 'grain of the voice', describes movement deep down in the cavities, the muscles, the membranes; the way the voice bears (out) the materiality of the body, with its checkings and releasings of breath. Simple breath holds no interest; the lungs are stupid organs. That graininess, for Barthes, inheres in friction, that sign of resistance: the body made manifest in the voice. As also in the hand as it writes. Rough breathing, then, is where writing, as well as speech, begins. Words must be shaggy as well as combed smooth.

Theodor Adorno, in an aside during a lecture in the 1950s, affirmed that the pure 'this-here' that art seeks to present cannot unfold in time or in space – 'all it can do really is take a breath'. Anything beyond that would be a betrayal. And yet we must keep breathing, must we not? And speaking. And writing. All language, poetry included, is a roughening of the breath.

Harry Gilonis

Introduction

by Philip Terry

A tall man stands atop a ladder. His hand reaches out and moves over the shelves of a bookcase, hovering over the poems of Kingsley Amis, brushing past several slim volumes by W.H. Auden, before alighting on a book by a relatively unknown poet, Tony Baker. The hand belongs to Harry Gilonis, who is working at the Poetry Society bookshop in Earl's Court. Here, at the end of each financial year, depreciation of stock had to be entered as an element of the accounts, so Gilonis found himself inspecting books for wear and tear from the top of a ladder. He started at 'A', and quickly found himself caught up short by his first acquaintance with Tony B-for-Baker and Richard C-for-Caddel, and many others (ending with Louis Zukofsky's *"A"*). As he climbed down the ladder to put aside more books to buy, he was discovering, not through peers or teachers but through impure serendipity, that interesting poetry wasn't just written by dead Americans. There was not only the post-Poundian, but the Objectivist and post-Objectivist, as well as the many English and Irish followers in that tradition, and it was a vibrant and living tradition at that.

Gilonis's interest in poetry began as a reader, not a writer, when, as it were, he went to school (like others before him including Basil Bunting) with Ezra Pound – the Ezuversity as it has sometimes been called. He spent a year reading the *Cantos* on the dole – an apprenticeship no longer available – using a university library ticket to access source books, from Provençal and Chinese dictionaries to books on art and architecture. After that he took the job at the Poetry Society bookshop. When, some time later, he began writing his own poetry, even collaborating with Tony Baker on some works, he began to produce poems that stand out in the sometimes insular English tradition as rich and strange. Here was a poetry that is radically open to other traditions and other poets across continents and across time, from William Carlos Williams to Li Shang-yin, from Trakl to Zukofsky, Lorine Niedecker and

Tom Raworth, and beyond poetry to the work of composers, of both classical and popular traditions, and of artists and thinkers, from Klee to Wittgenstein. The poetry is also characterised by an unusual openness to both traditional and emergent poetic forms such as visual, sound and performance poetry, and by a politics situated firmly on the Left. It is an *œuvre* that is vibrant, alive and full of possibility, with its eye set firmly on the future.

One of the early sequences included in this volume, 'cover versions', takes William Carlos Williams's poem 'This is just to say' and rings the changes in a set of variations, which render the poem not in, say, German or Italian, but as it might be written *in English* by a German or an Italian. The Portuguese version, for example, begins:

> that I ate
> the plums
> who were in
> icebox

The combined effect of these versions, like a verbal installation, makes the moment of Williams's poem ricochet across the Atlantic, from country to country, from fridge to icebox to cooler. This theme of variation and translation – which links back to Bach's *Goldberg Variations* and to Raymond Queneau and other Oulipians – is a key *modus operandi* in Gilonis's work (it is there also in the NORTH HILLS corpus and in 'Three Misreadings of Horatian Odes', and elsewhere), and it puts Gilonis at the head of a long line of innovative contemporary poets, from Tim Atkins to Peter Hughes and Caroline Bergvall, who have been engaged in renewing poetry with experimental, prismatic, forms of translation.

Other poems here engage with nature and the pastoral tradition. In the second of his 'two carnivore sonnets' Gilonis describes the speed, swoop and blur of the airborne predator, capturing its darting in the movement of the language:

> light on blur of wings
> only seen
> after its vanishing

The carnivore in question, *Cordulegaster boltonii*, the golden-ringed dragonfly, could have been the subject of a Ted Hughes poem, but the delicacy and precision of observation here, with its respect for the insect-other, makes Hughes's work seem almost bombastic in comparison. Another diptych, 'Two Poems from the English of the Wordsworths', gives us a different take on nature poetry. These pieces obliquely circle round Wordsworth's poem 'I wandered lonely as a cloud', in the first piece by sampling excerpts from Dorothy Wordsworth's *Journal* entry of 15 April 1805 describing the same episode (which Gilonis defamiliarises by removing any reference to 'daffodils'), in the second by performing erasures on Wordsworth's poem itself. Gilonis is attracted to the poem because, like the Wordsworths, he takes seriously the idea of writing about flowers, and in other poems, such as 'walk the line', his descriptive eye is arresting in its precision:

> on a far slower
> swell; sea
> -campion's white
> globular calices
> bright nodes shining
> on a ground of buff

It is typical of Gilonis to approach with new eyes a traditional poetic task such as this (he does much the same with the ekphrastic), to both pick up on and renew the tradition with experimental forms. Though the Wordsworths' work once helped lift the veil on nature, the tradition it established has, through repetition, become part of what, paradoxically, prevents us from seeing. There is nothing more clichéd than a poem about flowers.

Gilonis's meticulous use of language inspires meticulous reading. Many of his poems take delight in meaningful word-play, reminding us of the different senses hiding behind a single word, of words' homophones ('peace' and 'piece'), or the different words hiding in a single sequence of letters. In 'remembering Scott LaFaro' he writes, in an efflorescence of word-play reminiscent of Raworth:

```
            –   wind
        and light

        move the
        leaves

                day
        and night

        leave no
        moves
```

Such close attention to language, here and elsewhere, reminds us of the different layers and different senses packed into words. The effect is part of a larger de-sedimentation of the language, an exploding of linguistic hierarchies, through which the reader has a greater awareness of words' multiple senses, and the words in the poem, even its letters, begin to breathe. There is a linguistic turn here, but it is one that is simultaneously embodied, which is one reason why place plays such an important role in these poems. The suggestion is that attention to the signifier and attention to the world are not mutually exclusive, as some readings of structuralism have suggested, but folded together. The point is made succinctly in 'The Matter of Britain', each line literally part of the 'matter' of Britain – Natrolite, Opal, etc. – while, as an acrostic, the letters placed along the left-hand margin read: NO IDEAS BUT IN THINGS.

What this fails to convey is the sheer variety of poems and approaches here. Many begin with a musical theme, such as 'pibroch' (for Sorley Maclean): *pibroch*, a Scottish mode of piping, is a theme-and-variation form, and here Gilonis extemporises on the theme of Sorley Maclean's poem '*A' Chorra-Ghridheach*' ('The Heron') to magnificent effect. But there are also playful sound poems based on birdsong notation – 'Learning the Warblers' – experiments in concrete poetry such as 'an egg for E.', minimalist nature poems reminiscent of the work of Ian Hamilton Finlay and Thomas A Clark, such as 'WIND KEEN', which cry out to be carved in slate or cut into the side of a chalk hill; *ghazals*, shanties, re-visioning translations and misreadings, collaborations, and poems based on noun-plus-adjective combinations reminiscent of Queneau's *quennet*. And there are powerful performance and political poems, such as 'foreign policy', and *unHealed*, which creatively translates from the Welsh of the *Canu Heledd* ('long after the old Welsh', as Gilonis puts it):

> watcher wearied in tabu ringed
> a chant be in retch
> grown wrong duty
>
> wrath gadgetry threw way edgy
> a wrath eddy a wind ode
> wage idly war

Again working with variation, the poem progressively meta-morphoses this ancient lament into a fierce critique of coalition warmongering, here with lines taken verbatim from the 'corporate ethics' and other sections of the website of a company that manu-factured cruise-missiles used in Iraq:

> fully field programmable
> with in-flight re-targeting
> to cover the whole kill chain
>
> with sensor-to-shooter capability
> for effects-based engagement
> and an integral good-faith report

The volume and variety of poems collected here, combined with their linguistic depth, makes it impossible to discuss very many of them in great detail in an introduction. Yet what becomes in-creasingly clear as one reads is that this is a body of work of the highest ambition, and highest order. If all of English poetry of the last fifty years was suddenly lost from the archive, in the kind of textual catastrophe envisioned in Christine Brooke-Rose's novel *Verbivore*, one could go a long way towards reconstructing much of the best of it, and much of what matters about it in terms of the future of poetry, starting from the poems in this book. Read it. Then read it again.

Philip Terry

Rough Breathing

Catullus played Bach,

moving
with the
upbow &
the voice :

Schaue…
        hear
fiddle
playing clear

music

still(s)
       the
air, an
aria

under a
flaked arch

arco, light(s)
in air
       after
-noon, between
slab stone,
       before
the sixth hour
:
from the vault
saints &
prophets gaze
dispassionate ;

                    I did not
                    expect
                    this pattern
                       :
                    alert, such
                    particulars
                    elate, and   hurt

tears streaming
from the eyes:

o gods

grant me this thing

that song
bowed &
          fingered
giving itself
          after &
          beyond
          the words

               with
what grace
-notes,
          what
measure,

the song
set(s) free
:
a beginning, a
leap

a setting, a
placing
of the bow

    a small softness
    begins the stroke

the idea
is suffused
in light

marble swirl, and

Licht
-ung,
    the light
-ning –

  .

music   overhea(r)d

love
   /
      unclouding

the rose
in the stone
:
the un-
concealed –

a quick lift
of the bow

    the tone
    dies away

(*distance*
is not bridged
or abolished)

time
makes
melody

&

the rest
is   (a sign of
silence :

        … prati
ultimi flos;

Bach
read
Catullus

,

saw

a
small flower

at the   field's
edge

cut
by the share
and

unfolding

into

song

for my father, violinist

a song-sing

for Peter Quartermain

breathing
       the littoral:

an ammoniac air,

brine &
  iodine

ineluctable
         bladder's
wreck
     in patches
     on ledges
     on the side
     of the rock
              splashed
              with spray

swirling
        foam
lines
    the runnel
    branching
    slantwise
        down
        to the sea

[for Tony Baker]

      a
Feynman
       line

dividing
truth from lies:

the world divides…

"it is not put together
 cannot be put together

 states of affairs are not

 there are states that are"

from this
     posit
ion,
     posit
worlds

    that

Fall

      moving

  into

    place

cover versions

This is to be said (*Deutsches Gedicht*)	That is right to say (*Poesia italiana*)
fairly that I ate the plums Those were in icebox	that I have eaten Plums They were inside the icebox
and who you probably stored to the breakfast	is that probably you were saving for the first breakfast
me to forgive which was so cold them *köstliches* so sweet and were so cold	you pardon to me were therefore sweet and therefore cold exquisite
•	•

It is right to indicate
(*Poème française*)

that I ate
plums
which were in
the cooler

and which
you were probably
economy
for the breakfast

Forgive me that
they were so soft
and so cold
delicious

•

That's just to say
(*Poema português*)

that I ate
the plums
Who were in
icebox

and that
you it was conserving
probably
for the small thus delicious lunch

pardons me
that was thus cold
candy
and thus delicious

•

This is just to be said
(*Nederlands gedicht*)

I have eaten
The plums
those were in
They are freezing

and which
You probably were
Saving
for breakfast

Forgive me
They were delicious
so sweet
And so cold

.

This is just to say
(*Poema català*)

I ate
prunes
who were in
the fridge

and which ones
you are probably
savings
for *perdona* breakfast

forget me
were very sweet and delicious

so cold

.

28

Songbook 1

sound made
sound made
fairly hidden
(kind of) –

arrived at finally
he, she, it, that, these
on the island
in the river

for
the fine
the secluded
the

seeds and eggs,
bullets and shot –
good and superior
(indicates irony)

Consider it irregular
floating and variable
tall, long,
short –

left, right
left, right
flow, circulate
inferior, esteemed

for
the lovely,
the dark
the …

"in your waking
in your sleeping"
he (bracket
her) bracket

implore NOT
acquire NOT
can, may,
NOT be done;

awake,
asleep;
quiver, a dose
of medicine.

Far reaching and distant,
interrogative?
Anxious expletive –
to begin.

Turn half over, roll
on one side; turn
around, revolve,
turn back. Awry.

Consider it uneven
floating and variable
short, tall,
long –

left, right
left, right
variegated, bright
– one gathers.

For
the clear
the refined
the

dignified, numerous,
massive, dense –
grouped
together;

consider it a discrepancy
floating and variable
long, short,
tall –

left, right
left, right
selected (one gathers)
if you choose…

for
the obscure
the gentle
the

swelling music
to laugh at, take
pleasure in.
Final. Joy.

•

from a Hebridean notebook

a rabbit's shoulder blade folded into the sand

two carnivore sonnets

1. *Sympetrum sanguineum*

rapt-
or spun
fila-
ment,
blood-
crimson
ruddy
darter dart-
s in shafts
of sun,
sits so briefly
'black of
wing' in clou-
-ded shade

2. *Cordulegaster boltonii*

sunshimmer, sweat-
haze, glint as of
zebra-stripe &
boltonii dances,
'banded black', in-
to and out of
field of vision
in the same half-in-
stant, buzz-saw hum
of course inaudible
&
light on blur of wings
only seen
after its vanishing

5 Latin Poems

i)   moves

     ale

     late

ii)   super

     ore

     more

     late

viii) beat   interest

ix) latent

     graves

     bonus

     victor

xi) grave

     age

there is from every thing
an ephemeral resonance

electrons dance behind the eyes
gold dust moves   an ångström at a time

bow on stopped string
harmonic

wet finger on the rim
of a wet glass

dŵr clir a nos glir
falling upwards by stellated water

Orion
wheels over Llyn Peris

nothing there
but nothingness

and behind
the sound of the grass growing

Daruma

Daruma
"for good luck"
(•) one eye inked:

the wish ful
-filled, other
filled in (eye)

to see, be
stab(i)le:
symmetry.

remembering Paul Haines

the
tip
of the
small
pond
lit
by the
late
sun-
light

one is reminded
of nothing

Five Impromptus

bunched heads
-cow-
over the hedge
-parsley-

*

descending
       forth
the whistle to her dog
a unison with birdsong

*

self-coloured:

tiny white fly / white pampas-grass

two crows / shadow

*

ZETTEL, 199

crinkled
on the
gravel

sweet
paper
butterfly

*

one
lone
blue
bell

in a
pride of
dande-
lions

liquid (Cona
coffee)   bird
-call

distant radio

"breaking up/
          /making up"

clouds massing

morning

Two Poems from the English of the Wordsworths

1   When we were in the woods
beyond Gowborrow Park we
saw a few   close by the water-
side. The lake had floated
the seeds ashore.
As we went along   there were more
and yet more; and at last, under
the boughs of the trees,
a long belt   about the breadth
of a road.   I never saw them
so beautiful. They grew
among the mossy stones:
some rested their heads,
the rest reeled and danced,
laughed with the wind;
there were stragglers
a few yards   higher up
but so few   as not
to disturb the simplicity.

15 April 1802

2   lonely
high
once
golden
     beneath
and

continuous
and
  stretched
along
          a
             dance

waves
   sparkling
  not
    company:
     but
    show

         I
vacant
    inward
    solitude
     pleasure
dances

for Lorine Niedecker

reverse film:

see blade slide,
heal, seal lips
      of fissure
      to a fine line

dissection
in reverse:
  restoring
wholeness, but
  keeping the
clarity
, the seeing
      clear

start
with what
you know:
or
at least,
how little –

nothing else
but the small nouns,

the particulars:

not to talk
distantly,
not betray   those
who get made into crowds

but get at
that clarity:
not "thin,
thin", but clean,
clean and   **clear** –

a small eloquence,   dry
like fenugreek
on the tongue;

saying
that "a half-line is
in the line, that
a growing stalk
is wheat"

not
to reduce the thing
to nothing;
for being   is becoming
and I am
a verb,
a verb
buttressed
by things

to catch
the 'grain'
of things,

the detail, not
mirage, of
seeing:

– a vermicelli scatter
of seedhusks
on whorled cow
-flop, purple gleam

on glume of wood
melick, lichen
on river rocks
reniform in sunlight –

to find
in such attention **paid**
a warranty

that the small
makes manifest
the whole

Song for Annie

Follow the clews
and you will arrive at
something

we are not isolate, moving
without purpose
but "in the world;
for use, therefore ... worthwhile"

.

light through clouds
on the high hills
is not there
from or for our naming
but
will let us near

.

at the heart of it all
a quiet

.

a pause in the talk
a caesura in the lovemaking
and
my eye scans feet
body rests

the act of poetry,
not the art

.

and my song: take care, o

    <u>take</u>
    care

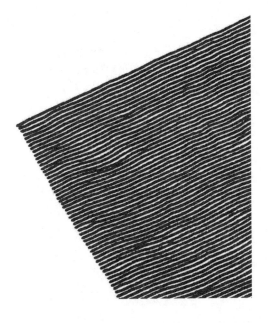

(from) Axioms

"cunning in music and the mathematics"
The Taming of the Shrew

I

lovely, or
lonely

moving
tentatively

wanting to describe
not explain

the cadences
are found

at the same time
the measure

and the thing
measured

the line is there
before we draw it,

dancing
mathematics;

not frozen
calculi

but the moving
edge

the ascent
of empty space

laying down
a path

a bell ringing
in the empty sky

the geography
has to be described

the movement
of the mechanism

successive
addition

notes
graced, enriched

fragile
elements;

so as to seek the laws
that cause the song:

"always it renewed
　　its clear tone; always

　　there was a fresh cut
　　from which the song

　　issued,
　　sap from a bough"

these notes
moved the stones

II

melody
affirmed and denied

disorder
flows

the changing noise
must have an effect

for what themes
have *no* point? and

what process *is*
knowing how to go on?

sticking to the bottom,
deep as you can get –

descriptions
are misleading:

'the impression
 of a picture-duck

incorporated in the song
implicit in the movement

you can almost hear it,
a duck calling your name'

[*there are constant lapses*
from description into explanation here;

and 'understanding' is
a vague enough concept]

miscalculating
is the key,

the song
a kind of irruption,

eruption,
interruption

caught
in this net of language

surprised
at the turns it takes

rapid,
gliding

IV

some kind of image
of an endless row

the axiom
of choice

you don't understand
any more of a rule

than
you can explain

our disease
is wanting to explain

a description
the solution

of
the difficulty

"you cannot view a landscape
as a whole

moving in it
so slowly

you forget one part
when you come to another"

form
is what makes it graspable

the construction
compels acceptance

linked,
in a form

additive
process

changing
with every new proportion

the series
is infinite:

the proof
is a *path*

an allusion
to something outside,

it does not
mention itself:

a long
sine-wave,

a song
sung on the border,

versatile then,
now immobile –

an
endless technique

and a small
coda

VI

structured and
economical

angled slopes,
discontinuity

there is no entity,
only change

a thicker base beneath
folds and breaks

the valley
undrowned

a new form
has been found

it must begin anywhere
and continue

"the descriptions which suggest themselves
are all misleading"

what is proved
is withdrawn from doubt

axiom:
self-evident principle

as it
falls apart

there's a temptation
to say more

when everything
has been described

(*not the result,*
but that we reach it)

why bother
about an end?

'so far there is no such thing
as an answer to your question'

i.m. Steve Lacy

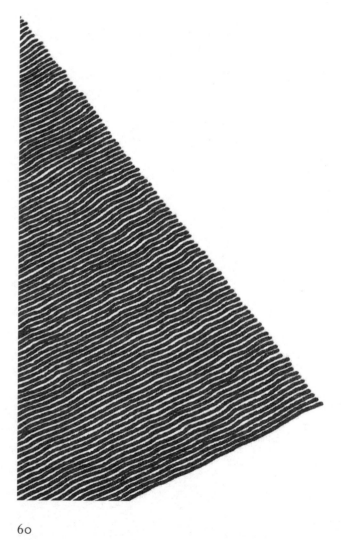

on the white
grass not the Object
but the light

where my feet
would have notched
its blades

not the dew but
a pool
of moon

Theory

the cracks
in an old wall,
the shape
of a cloud,
the path of
a falling leaf
or the froth
on a pint of beer

lines for David Bellingham
(*and in memory M. E. S.*)

once repetition is empty
it is empty, repetition
say, is empty repetition
repetition once empty is
empty, is it repetition
is it, say, repetition
once repetition is empty
repetition is empty it
is empty, say, repetition

Descant on a Theme by Brian Coffey

鶼 *chien*: a fabulous bird with one eye and one wing, a pair
must unite in order to fly. [*doubled*] a pair – man and wife

Mathews' Chinese-English Dictionary

"In parable chinese fictive one-winged birds
that fly together as one each lifting other"

Brian Coffey, *Advent* II

one-eyed &
one-winged
they fly
as one together

leg joined with leg in
pure winged linking,
each wing with wing
of an other, reflecting

in the air
suspendat
hirundo
with
"unwearied affection"

each
by other taught

each
lifting the other

light and easy
they tumble in the air

they float
on the spring wind
they bring
the spring

elthe, elthe
chelidon

swirling glide
over scrub-oak & juniper
'sunny gulleys
in the mountains'

skimming low
over water,
dipping, sipping
its surface

twin beaks
            scooping
ephemer
        -optera
dipping
        over
river
      glitter

chittering song
of two as one

tsink, tsink
tswit, tswit,
tsi-kuk

thin singing
   in
empty colonnades

gliding
    in
failing wind

looped, linked
with a cord
of light, they
swoop, sink;
in accord,
they alight

settling
in the osiers
of an eyot
on the river

over white sand
under black pines
in slant light

under cold moon,
willow-cotton
snow on snow

at the lake's edge
ringed by winter
all fly together

"and after
a most sweet
singing

submerge themselves
and rise again
in spring

from far away

a 100-stanza renga

(odd-numbered stanzas: Harry Gilonis; *even-numbered stanzas, Tony Baker*)

1   Fern sits in the shade
    where we wallow   green
    and thoughtless

2   in the shadows fired
    with thirst midst
    slack willows what-
    stand-well &
            truly rooted

3   behind the trees   water   falls
    TO THE HILLS —> peaty ghylls
    run in tiers   on black fell moss
    Ure feet from Eden

4   …his ship towards –
         "sailed uphill –"
    annihilating each fixed star

5   the Leonids sputter & hiss, Rigel
    bobs at the masthead: *le navire*
    est dans la lumière, lovely
    on the water –

6   leaf-choked –
dank grass beneath our bruised feet

7   a blue moon. nightblue apple trees.
star-naked boys in the meadow.
a frog. a leaf. a fire-fly. leaves.

8   asking myself: how come these things pile up at my door?
answering: & do not the weeds too have right of access to the sun?

9   there's no light under the orchard,
under the hill; above, just the glimmer
      of *Minuartia verna*

10 a waste and howling wilderness
this window open in
      to the infernal world

11 How long shall I heare the sighs and groanes
O Tythes, Excize, Taxes, Pollings &c
This government is firmly committed to

12   brute strength   hauled up
     "dark matter", undetectable, nameless
     names burnt against the wall the

13   petals blowing row on row,
     roots that clutch a-
     midst the stubble of Flanders fields

14   frost-wrecked

     stalks dug in
     every part   the bright hectic

     tubby cotyledons

15   "in an inferior world"
     in a laich wind
     bog-cotton's tiny cumuli
     snipe tumble drumming

16   drumming in   an inferior

     world thunders at the tunnel-mouth the approaching
     magnates, lutenist, apoplectic, fish-man

     all gone beneath the mountain

17   a crevasse in the sky blue light under the black hill

by the frozen water eyelids locked in frost

cold sickle-moons in the boot-tops

18   …migrants

at the light-ship…

19   between the poles   at the lagoon's edge
"we two together…" under Orion
     swimming in black water

20   – breaks over
our bed of scruffy heather

21   the shadow of young girls and flowers
asleep on the broom-filled hill

22   doped air thick with cinders,
the scorching desire for
We
have become the market
& the market's need all-consuming

23 Who will sell
        this wonderful morning
    and the air that we breathe
        EVERYTHING REDUCED
    a strong force, a single theory

24   for the infinitely
                        small or large
        & another for

    fireflies brief oceans the unaccounted for the

25 unvisible –
            "seen the hills and they were just –"
            "seen one tree and you've seen –"

                            the fern's signature
    in the coal, the new bracken's crozier –

26   the warbler in the osier –

            o nothing could be finer
            wotchercock, sang the mynah

27 'Dinah' sung in the Public,   chalk dust by the darts mat,   flat
    beer & talk ebb & flow, going down on the cards,   in the yard
    by the cludgie   falling drunkenly upwards into a pool of stars

28   our drenched words
                    still cling to   as spores…

    If one could listen at the sound of their falling
    would make a music uneclipsable, before   & after ours

29   the houses wheel over the earth
     stars   sporadic   No music
     from these spheres

30   where silence is, the other night
     a gay stream tripped –
     I seasonally adjust myself:
     put on more clothes

31   "ottim time – an' the livs is fallin' – "
     with such easy loss of innocence
     the trees shed their leaf aprons

32   without strings, mountains, junk, floating free
     up the river   that we are
     free agents
     in the want of, wanting rid of it

33   the island used up, "the sea
      which is death", a river
      aflame   orange
      what forests perish from sick effluviums

34   what tree burgeons over sterile earth –
      not a mushroom gathered
                    this rainless summer

35   hot like a stove in the desert night
      moon's not silver but yellow
      splashes on our skin
      parched as earth, hungrier

36   for love,
          for one full hull charged
          with the weight of us,
              of each our stowing

37   at rest, buoyant
      entangled
      in lilies

38 on the water-pools
    we delve in
    ridiculously familiar

39 below the water-line
    kelp used for glass & soap :
    & rent charged
    for the land under the water

40 the ten authorities
    permanently poised
    in comfort your own home

41 in time
    this fainful bsiness
    will will soonfeul soon
    will soon be onert

42
    [leave
    this
    space
    blank]

43 moving across the water
    black and grey   meet at the horizon
    in a kind of dancing light
    water drips from the vertical oars

44 to salute a botched job
    sluiced silence   for fifty years
    convincement in the magnitudes of stars

45 in quiet sitting, in the bronze
    of the bracken   the star
    arises   Altair in your hair

46 after all these years
    six new moons, blue & crazy
    paved frost on a rubble-filled heap 'dop'
    for a brambly

47 rainheavy and pissed on by the *púca* – splats –
    rips web – *De lineis insectabilibus* only house
    unless it rains – tatters – Brier Spider
    unhoused – ditto *Oonops* in my teapot

48   cupped hillocks tripped up a rip-off
      off Stoops gnatty in a downpour where
      lights collapse to loop the nightslope

49   stoked Aga smoke slopes up back
      ice is crisp on the steps up to the Miners'

      seems there are faults, reserves exhausted

      and a flower frozen on the window, morning

50   dark as night
                    covered in this
                    black stuff

      men drift away: the hills don't
          stay either – shiftless, insufficient

51   they drift in the current
      coated in black gurry
      beyond prejudice   or reason
      will we talk about the black birds?

52   will we suffer exoneration?
      will we scrape a living from the pipelines?
      & who is there of the herring-smacks will play pibroch?

53 no-one hears the small music; the wind
    in the whin, the flights of warblers,
    the sedge's humming drone; nor, tiny thunder,
    the birl, the dirl, the skirl of the *urlar* of the heather

54 nor kittling of dwarfish house-mice
    (nest best in the hessian of cold meat stores,
    little mountains of fur & feather)

55 t follow the harrow a hell-fr-leather *perr–yu–weet* plummet

56 slapdash to let loop the old
    leaves drip groundward

57 each one treeless
    but each fungus home
    to generations of worms
    "fruit not void of utilitie"

58 for the wine thrives by patience
    & the wise man asks not
            wherein his soul shall be clothed…

(coloured bulbs dance at the entrance to the pier…

59 and there is light crowning the thorns of the wire
    and the crossbeams   and the shined metal

    aligned & twisted skyward
    for a day of howling

60 stark carcass bottomless
    stripped to the pitstone. Spit
    pith & decorous.

    "for the fire fox must cross the great water"

61 lit by fox-fire and Artemisia
    round three peaks
    "derived from Definitive Maps"
    bring lavender home from the moor
    its roots & ours intertwined

62 upon the skirts
    of Ingleborough Hill   snowed tofts
    dug, thence scarred, now unheard of

63 a little north of Folly
    pine under a duvet of
    snow   humped snouts aside of
    smouts   walling moving up a
    beacon   moon

64   above the frith, contemplating
Solomon in all his tory
lands &
the distempered economics of unlabouring hands

65   that sweat be converted into ease
that the sun shine at night-time

66   that the topters fall not on my allotment
that the glow-worms, especially those of Lathkill, be not
                                extinguished

67   the sodium night-light does not dispirit
golden it glows into a new day

68   brings groundsel & pappus-dust:
that we are   as they are, our

                           outer lungs
suck carbon from milked air

69   …how and whether the Being of animals is constituted by
                          some kind of 'time'…
…how and where the Being of animals is constituted by some
                           kind of 'time'…
the curlew held level with our eyes in the headwind on Yellow
                                   Rigg
the wrens fucking in the Dentdale hedgerow

70   how and whether the animals of Being are constituted by any
                          kindness whatsoever...
     quarried limepits filled and dumped in—chewed shrewhead
                          on the threshold:

71   shew forth pitiful   & busily unkind
     we ofttimes do: & yes
     the grassblade purposes
     beyond our bodies' crushing it

72   sweet vernal, to unfold again & come
     upon the lawns that hold whatever is
     this loveliness you press me to

73   bittersweet, separated & entangled
     what laws we hold each other to;

     once   in spring light   inside you   on a fellside

74   (or twice   in night's shade
     the full moon on Moel Eilio)

75   Hell's Mouth lies behind Butlin's
     rubble piled up by the storm we call progress

76 ketchup-stained panels smashed
all at sea, sea-
beat   enough   more
and more's not enough

77 adrift in an ecliptic
Mécanique Céleste (Clough
wood waves shifts   blue sky &
bells in flower rippling

78 bob up & down, eight-
man made hares, spheres, beers
overhearing "is it here
        they still ring the curfew?"

79   or here the curlew
sings from knoll
a passing day

80 leaves the world
peeps
through to darkness
& forest coleoptera

81   spring is late   & delays
      the parson's mackerel w/ gooseberries

      cultivation is the root

82   taps the wild
      thorn's fruit
               & bindweed
      clings against the gardener

83   convulsed, eyes a
      gape   in no *agape*
      my cat & her husband:
      what a barbed thing   that arrow is

84   through-shot & in throes of
      hills greenish sheen
      eating what we are   in full
      colour detail of a treatment works

85   Spurned   and standing into danger
      the great tankers float by
      the coyote pisses on the *Wall Street Journal*

86 acid strips the eyes'
                  lights burning
       a stock of words we cannot hold / be held
  by, why
  John Deth you be not still –

87 [arm *del.*] [grasp *del.*] [clasp *del.*]
  [hand *del.*] [shoulder *del.*]
  [knee *del.*] [form *del.*] [smile *del.*]
  in the forests
  of the night

88 oubutts   dermestes

    unsheltered in the day's
    blaze skinned to crisps

89 "even bishops are 80% water"

    the burn untouched by seed-head stars
    we trace its restless calligraphy
    cross-rolling skewed & varicose

90 written / on the sky / *i cardellini*
    shivered windbells / off thistlescruff
    high Peak fields / not Central Park

91   stalk a skeletal wisp
         dry   a little prickly
      expel superfluous melancholy
         under Saturn and Mars
      & a jaundiced quarter-moon

92   too soon gone
      under cloud   the particular

      people I fear the loss of

      clarity to say it to watch a moth slap
      half the window, this furious
      slow shrinkage

93   we learn not to live with,
      learning to move
      under grave trees
      jagged and incomplete

94   systems crash: one dies, another
      dies about my ears —
                           a dustbin
      fires ashflakes on the air, the sense
      unfinished, of conversations hanging in mid-air

95   "time for a dog's-nose?"
"– high time." – and nothing more to say,
just to walk across a moor at sunset,
crepuscule   with Nellie and John –

96 hammering the keyboard into silences
between fought-for notes, ploughed bright
                                    & light

across the April fells

97   brightness falls
and the lark's shadow moves
searching for me, blindly,
across the hills

98   solo
               above no
      man's land

99   one bright harebell in flower

         one person facing another

100   committed to ebb
              the shadow
      your sweet mouth
          still clings to

The Matter of Britain

for Richard Caddel

Natrolite
Opal

Ilmenite
Dunstone
Edingtonite
Alstonite
Serpentine

Barytes
Umangite
Toadstone

Ilvaite
Nadorite

Tourmaline
Haematite
Idocrase
Nepheline
Gypsum
Sphalerite

Win(s)ter Songs

1.   in airslurry,
       in halfhail
               & the
       mountain *is*,

       sign and sight

       streams
             flow
       -ers
         thin out
       as you get
       higher

2.   clouds pulse
       and clear (sky)

       shadows flicker
       (as) eyelids close

3.   a bag
         (poly-
       thene) snap
       -ped from a roll
       to hold 'snap', a
       roll
         off each
       booted foot, the
       road's camber

4. rain in
   the neck, in-
   to another –

   each drip drops
   through s-
   trata to touch –

5. water's
            sough,
   rain
   's sign
            bows
   over
   rain too
   over the
   roof-ridge

   in tune

6. drop drupe
   on twig quickens
   to brightness
   silverquick

   from arborescence:

7.   nimbus.
   shouting
   at nothing, spats
   of rain

   go, slowly

   all is less than true

8.   the old term, frankly:
                              pea-soup,
                    misty mornings,
          simple motion, the old
          tune, the
                air

9.   foot
     de-
              press
     -ed
     on the
     ground,
                daily
     grind,
                    not
     across a field

10. hill figures
            prefigured
     dust
             in the throat
     the word 'water'
     thirst
               for the word
     the word
     yes
     merely spoken
     this morning

11. cloud
            across
       land,
               pleats
       folded
               on
       folds

               valley
       streams
               away

                    for Tony, Liz & Liam

three, plus a distant relation

in direct spring light
the dust is slightly cooler
where the hooves have been

•

such thirst conjured up
by slick dark green bramble leaves
weighed with cuckoo-spit

•

birch scrub burnt off &
downwind air freighted with dust
smelling of nutmeg

• •

a stumble
shifts a rock
putting the beck
out of tune

content[1] fitting
form[2]:

    hares
at a field's
edge

content[3] fitting
form[4]:

    hares
at a field's
edge

Concise Oxford Dictionary

1: content[1] *n.* 3 constituent elements of a conception: opp. *form*
2: form[1] *n.* 4 mode in which thing exists or manifests itself:
    cf. CONTENT[1]
3: content[2] *n.* contented state, satisfaction
4: form[1] *n.* 14 hare's lair

Learning the Warblers

1   **grasshopper warbler** (*Locustella naevia*)

pit . pitt . pitt pitt . whitt .
chik . tchick . twhitt . twitt .
tschek tschek .

2   **sedge warbler** (*Acrocephalus schoenobaenus*)

tuc . tucc . tuck . tuctuctuctuc .
tsrr . trr . trrr . karr .
tsek .

3   **marsh warbler** (*Acrocephalus palustris*)

tac . tschak . tuc . tchuc . chuck .
twitt . vit . tweek . tic-tirric .
zawee . za-wee . churr .
st-t-t . ᴢɪCHEH ᴢi-CHEH . stit .

4   **reed warbler** (*Acrocephalus scirpaceus*)

kra .
vit .
crik-crik-crik . chara-chara-chara . jag-jag-jag .
chirruc-chirruc . chirruc-chirruc-chirruc . churuc-churuc-
    churuc-jag-jag-jag .
skurr . tchar . churr . churr-churr-churr . churrur-churruu .
trett trett trett tirri tirri tirri trü trü .
tere-tere-tere-cheerk-cheerk-tsair-tsair-twee-twee-twee .

5 **dartford warbler** (*Sylvia undata*)

tchurr . churr . chirrr . tchirr . tchirrr . tchir-r .
cherrr-tk . tchir-r-tuc-tuc . chaihrr-er . jer-jit .
gee-ee-ip .
tuk . tuc . chuck .
tak .

6 **lesser whitethroat** (*Sylvia curruca*)

tellellellellellellellell . tac-tac . tac . tacc-tacc . tacc . tak . tack .
chek . tchurr . chr-r-r-r . charr . chikka-chikka-chikka .
chay-de-de-de . chakakakakaka .
tett .

7 **whitethroat** (*Sylvia communis*)

dji-do ji-do ji-do ji-do ji-do . vit vit vit .
wheet . whit . whett-whett-whett . whit-whit-whit . hwett-
   hwett-wit-wit .
charr . churr . tcharr . tchurr . chairr . churrr . churrit .
tschek . tschack . check . tacc .
chuck .

8 **garden warbler** (*Sylvia borin*)

ooit . whit .
churr . tchurr-r-r . chur chur chur chur chur . tsharr .
check . check, check . check-check . chek-chek-chek . tacc-tacc .
   tacc . tack .
CHUCK-a-ro-CHE, CHUCK-a-ro .
chuck .

9 **blackcap** (*Sylvia atricapilla*)

deedeedee . deela-deela-deela .
tau-tau . tett-ett-ett-ett .
churr .
tak . tack . tac, tac . tac-tac . tzek .

10 **wood warbler** (*Phylloscopus sibilatrix*)

diuhdiuhdiuhdiuh . dee-ur . dee-you . duuh .
whit, whit, whit . vitvitvit . whit-whit-whit . stip-stip-stip . whit .
pip-pip-pip .
sip-sip-sip-sipsiprrrrr .
stip, stip, stip, stip-stip-stip-shreeee .
peeoo . pee-ou . peu . pew . piu . püü . pew-pew-pew-pew .
piu piu piu piu piu piu piu piu piu piu piu piu piu piu piu piu
    piu piu piu piu .
sip .

11 **chiffchaff** (*Phylloscopus collybita*)

houeet . hoot . hweet .
zip-zap . siff-siff-siff . tsiff-tsiff-tsiff .
chiff . chaff . chiff, chiff, chaff, chiff, chaff . chiff-chaff .
chiff chaff chaff chip chap chiff chep .
chirr-chirr . churr .
teet-teu . twit .

12 **willow warbler** (*Phylloscopus trochilus*)

hooeet . hoo-eet . too-eet .
titi-dje-djoo-dooee-dooi-djoo .
sooee . sooeet-sooeetoo .

13 goldcrest (*Regulus regulus*)

see . tsee . tsee-tsee . tsee-tsee-tsee . see-see-see . see-see-see-
    see . zi-zi-zi . zee-zee-zee .
see-see-see-see-sississi-sip .
stit-it-stir-te . sree-sree-sree-sree .
zi-zi-zi-zeee-zeee-zeee-zi-zi .
zi-zi-zi-zeee-zeee-zeee-zeee-zi-zi .
sise sisee sisee sesee seritete .
seeter-seeter-seeter .
cedar-cedar-cedar-cedar-sissu-pee .
zi .

14 firecrest (*Regulus ignicapillus*)

zit . zit-zit . peep . peep-peep .
seeseeseeseeseeseesirrr .
si-si .
tsee .

for P.C. Fencott

Some Horatian Ingredients

(*for Erica and Simon*)

plenty of
garlic,

a few
words

•

(*for Geoffrey and Valerie*)

some white
space

with bay
leaves

set in
it

•

northern *ghazal*

clear sky, no moon,
and Orion shining like a son-of-a-bitch.

hare's breath.
hair's breadth.

spicules of frost
on the *Deschampsia flexuosa*.

some (of *forty*) *fungi*

field mushroom (*Agaricus campestris*)

"let's go buy some real ones"

     – there's no need,
the sloping field
where we found
the sheep's skull by
sweet Hesleyside
    is alive
with skully lumps
      each bone-white
& slippery
with dew

penny bun (*Boletus edulis*)

"wolf's onion":
– swyne rotteth them vppe –
stem robust, cylindrical, pallid,
with slightly raised veins;
    bulbous clod
    mycorrhizal
    w/ spruce:
    flesh flushed
    dirty straw,
    or vinaceous

chanterelle (*Cantharellus cibarius*)

    girolles, abri-
    côte – sheltered
    on the hill's
    side
    :
    eschew
            the decay,
    & chew;

    wat'ry-yellow
    peppery
    quality,
    hot in an om'-
          -lette, cold
        tomato fold-
    ed in

velvet shank (*Flammulina velutipes*)

    by Watch Crags,
    out of the teeth
    of a north-easter,
    snow crescents
    in the boot-tops
    and sleet sat
    in the eyebrows

        to eyeball
        yellow
        light
          between
            spruces,

    sprucing them up:

orange birch bolete (*Leccinum versipelle*)

hunting with
stomachs,
with eyes

at the margins
of aspen
and grassland:

speckled stipes
tufted, tubes
mouse-grey;

under the fell
where the short-
eared owls

weren't, you
were
– but fly-et!

blewit (*Lepista saeva*)

near misled
by leaves
into missing it:

glutinous cap-top
with an unknown leaf of an
unknown tree glued on

and, under the clump,
blue legs,
tho' it be
warm autumn

oyster fungus (*Pleurotus ostreatus*)

found in the
skull of a
stranded whale

reversing decay
on rotten
logs

turning mul-
tiple rumps
to the moon

small scallops
from a
bough

casseroled
in
béchamel

dung roundhead (*Stropharia semiglobata*)

all
round
coming down
Cautley Spout,

so slen-
der &
pen-
dent
on
sheep
-shit:

golf
tees,

tiny
trees

rain-
washed
&
foot-
mashed,

hemi-
spheri-
cally
capped

& hued
by
falling
spores

Pelagic

Ἀθήνη / φήνη εἰδομένη [*Ody.*, III.371–372]

the sea moves
like music,
knowing no
fixed point;

no true
pole star
that must be had
showing

*

wind
moves sea
into laced
swell;

crests
slice air,
foam,
and surge;

white lines
'f gulls streak,
strike, stroke
the breakers;

waves
roll
in s l o w
glass-

bead breakage,
with cullet
of spin-
-drift…

*

a cobalt-
blue eye
with a clear
pale iris

cold and
arresting,
'without the good
of intellect…'

*

the world
and life,
one;

and the
ocean's
maxim, that

a meaningless sign
is
useless:

yet gannet massing
show a herring-
shoal,

the whole sky
filled & whitened
by them;

the plunge
of feathers'
oiled sheen,

of diving
blades, as
massed bubbles

of milky wake
rise and
burst

before
their green
surfacing…

*

blue shadows
on blue
water;

the sky
wave-
blue;

light
gave them wings
to follow

glistening
waves
in a state

of grace-
fulness
annulling space…

*

the wind's song sung
through a gull's
hollow bone;

"consciousness
is not a wave"
said Ruskin,

mind moving
over light, over air,
over water…

for David Connearn

The Inscriptions

for Carl Rakosi

for Anthilla
            and for Archedike
Hediste and
            Hegesilla
Kallipe,
        Kleophonis,
                    Melo
        (written   sgraffito)

Mnesilla
        Rhodopis
and Sime

who are
        beautiful
            &
        forgotten

Window, Light Outside

to make
        is to risk
making
a botch:

– 'forgiveness,
      horse!',
that I hazard
anything,

abolishing
chance
by chancing
my arm,
      not making
      head
and/or
      tail,

hand
      fallen back,
nothing
      made
through
  courting incapacity;

        instead,
assaying saying
the little
that one man
      reden kann:

to speak
            of a window,
light outside
        falling in   on
lime-washed walls,
eight lights
            thrown
across the floor;

or of
        seeing *Myosotis*,
water forget-me-not,
blue
        by a
small
        bridge,
water
        flowing
away,
        fleshy
stalks
        fringing
banks
where the shade
        of willow
and alder
            is not
too deep;

or saying again
what
has been expressed:

as how,
in the south,
"trees' leaves
turn with the year,
but only the oldest
            fall…":

this
        not
the
    'appearance
        of truth'
but
    truth's
appearance:

truth, which is
        prefixed
by privation,
                ἀ-
λήθεια,
            dis-
covery;

            in
brevity
        to risk
obscurity,
            seeing
meaning
        in a
single
        magpie

over
    an
en-
    filade
of
   trees
in
   early
morning,
     September
sun,
  white
&
  black
     alike
alight
      in
sun's bright
fire…

here
is no
concern
with 'ornament';

      it is
enough
to have
  an "earthen
      jug,

self-
supporting,
            a
thing"
        set
in
     space,
it-
    self
   itself,   .

giving
          a shape
to the void
              around it
as music
             does
to silence;
           a jug
tactile
        as a
lemon,
          as succinct
and un-
            obscure
as a
          Braque –

as a bowl
             of fruit, a
guitar,

glasses
and a bottle
of wine, set
  on a table,
readied
          for
 companionship,
outlined
       in the room
by windowed
        light;
all here
     invites:
'touch,
     smell,
drink
    and play…'

each thing seen
     itself,
          as
cats fucking,
   mewing like
buzzards, the
male's penis
studded

with pointed,
     horny
spikes, a
     barbed
Cupid's arrow;

as White's
           wasp's
      eyes, "lunated
in a
      crescent"…

clear
      seeing,
each word
                differing
as a leaf
         from
its neighbour,
                   turning
in air, in
         incessant
motion,
            once
         in an eye-
blink,
         pale
underside
         twisting
         in tiny
breeze;

'had they been
         tougher,
harder,
            more durable,
more valuable,
                   things
would be different'

each
           word
       in limited,
limiting clarity
           showing
the World,
               an
ideal,
       inescapable,
variegated
               variety;

to walk
           into
the poem,

               to see
sun   on sea
               through
the cloister
               door-
way.

Reading Hölderlin on Orkney

… as people
are fond of presences, I have come to
see you, you Islands, and you,
you mouths of streams …

Friedrich Hölderlin, *Die Wanderung*

I

islanded:
  and here, at a
burn's mouth be-
tween hills
facing ocean, days
chasing days…
  What a riddle
to pose,
here or any-
where, what
might be **pure
of origin**? (As if
that was, or
could be, of
moment, at
these moments, with
the drifting of
sleet, of birds,
whose wing
beats estab-
lish the only
measure…)

But a question, still,
that song **schooled
by skylarks**
might answer
if it met
the clear light
by the Burn
of Stourdale,
its water wind-
feathered and
light
as a kitti-
wake, blown
off a cliff
into ocean

11

wind on water, *allegro*
light on water, *legato*
wind on water, *vivace*:

and a window, open
to light
off the sea, from the sky

with, above, **a roof
smoke blossoms from**

and, outside, turf,
daisied
with hailstones,

where snow
holds the place
of shadow

III

under clouds,
peace; under
pieces of cloud
the sunlight
makes its way
up the slack of the hill,
over myrtle
and heather
that the Atlantic
dots with foam…
In an inshot of spray
the sea breathes
up the *geo*,
and the hill,
the cliff, looms;
cloud is cut
by its edge, a
near horizon,
and the air's flecked
with fulmars,
their impure joy
the "consciousness
of necessity", of
the world, ready-
to-hand and **hard**
to grasp…
As snow,
half-gleaming,
signifies, **the light,**
benevolent, is
reluctant to flower;

scattered to lucency
by salt in the air,
scattered to web,
to trace, to skein,
to haze…

IV

In Berriedale,
goldcrests, they say,
and woodsong

can be
within
hearing;

in this deep valley
what   might not
be forgotten

in the shade
of woods, far
from the burn of light

V

On the Howes of Quoyawa, on
the Knap of Trowieglen, fish-
bone-widths of **snow**
silver in the sunlight:

to move, pathless, among rocks
and heather, aflame with
quiet fire; **to trace**
the course of streams,

to learn to tell
white hare
from white boulder,
the specific

names like morning breezes
– and their absence, too, cooling
as the un-named lochan's
slaty water…

On the crags
by the Burn of the Kame,
the bare stones
of language:

under that dark light
no word
like 'flower'
will flower…

here, twin slabs of rock,
and it clear that, once,
a rocking-
stone sat,

poised, local,
wavering
between the total
and the particular,

set wobbling
by the weight
of the immanent
moment,

by thought
rocked
as if settled
on water:

on a mountain
on a slope
on a hill

adrift
in un-
certain sea

without ebbtide
without oar
without rudder

VI

restless,
the burns,

the wind,
the tide;

lazier,
light

fades
into night,

into
cloud's

radiant
haze

and tulli-
menting stars

...both buoyed and clever
but cross-grained, lop-
sided to manage: turning
round and round the man-
œuvre she was best at, little
and dancing, sea-tossed;

she seemed to find her head again –
though even a small change
in the disposition of her weight
produced violent changes
in her behaviour;

how immensely tall
everything looked
from my low station
in the coracle...

Pibroch

for Sorley Maclean

I am only that Job in feathers, a heron, myself
Hugh MacDiarmid, 'Lament for the Great Music'

urlar

a heron landing
on top of sea-wrack
folding wings
attending what's near

on stones of the ebb-shore
seeing slippery ocean
hearing sea swallowing
brine chafing pebbles

seeing cold water
listening to uproar
breaking on slabs
a restless sea

ath-ruith [thumb-variation/theme]

heron
on wrack
folding wings
attending

on an ebb-shore
seeing ocean
hearing sea
chafing pebbles

seeing water
hearing uproar
on slabs
the sea

siubhal

a grey heron landing
on top of sea-wrack,
folding wings
attending to what's near

on stones of an ebb-shore,
seeing the slippery ocean;
hearing the sea swallowing,
and brine chafing pebbles

seeing the cold water,
listening to beach uproar;
breaking on slabs,
the restless sea

leumluth

a demure heron landing
lowering her legs
on top of sea-wrack,
maroon and vile-smelling;
folding her wings close
– neat, quite fastidious –
attending to what's near

on the bare stones of the ebb-shore
above the tide-line,
seeing the slippery ocean
light-patterned, netted;
hearing the sea swallowing
- gutteral, glottal -
and brine chafing pebbles

seeing the cold salt water
of a cut-off lochan,
listening to beach uproar,
slap of water on water;
breaking on flat slabs
– raised beach or skerry –
the restless sea

taorluath

a demure grey heron landing
lowering her long legs
atop scattered sea-wrack,
midged, maroon and foul-smelling;
folding her wide wings close,
neat, if not fastidious,
and attending to what's near her

on the bare stones of the ebb-shore
above the tide's kelp-line,
seeing the slippery ocean
bright-light-patterned and fretted;
hearing the throated sea swallow
gutterally, glottally,
and its brine chafe at pebbles

seeing the cold trembling water
of an arm of a sea-loch,
listening to the beach uproar,
percussive slapping of water;
breaking headlong on slabs
of raised beach or skerry
is the restless sea

Crunnluath [crown-variation]

a demure grey heron landing limber
lowering long legs and brown feet sluggishly
to alight on a spot she'd once arisen from
on wave-scattered bladder-wrack,
midgy, maroon, slimy, foul-smelling;
compactly folding widths of wings close,
neatly, fastidiously, leaving her free
to turn an eye's yellow iris
to attend to what's near her

on the bare pale gneiss of the ebb-shore
above the syzygied spring-tide's
storm-blurred kelp-line,
with the sun descending a flame of wrath:
seeing the ocean, slippery, reticulate,
bright, light, and speckle-patterned;
hearing the sea's weeded throat
stuttering, swallowing, glottal and gutteral,
spitting at froth, its brine chafing at pebbles

seeing the tremulous salt-packed sea-cold water
of a lochan's inlet cut off from the loch,
listening to the noise of each agile wave
in its rising, its falling, and its swift rebounding,
each reach of beach's reverberating roaring,
percussive slapping, water on water, as spray cascades;
and – breaking headlong on craggy slabs
of ceaselessly battered raised beach or skerry –
are the dark deep waves of the restless sea

urlar

a heron landing
on top of sea-wrack
folding her wings
attending what's near

on the stones of the ebb-shore
seeing the slippery ocean
hearing sea swallowing
and brine chafing pebbles

seeing cold water
listening to uproar
the breaking on slabs
of the restless sea

for Michael Finnissy

air's susurrus
through the rushes:

the gaps matter
as much as the stems,

the stalks, all
quavers in the wind

Song 9

and their hands, the way
they hold their hands,
pianists I mean, in
the pauses, poised, held,
in a way thought
could only default,
still, as a leaf
curled as it dried,
or a crab's shell
upright on shingle

for Ian Pace

Afar / Alongside

Afar

for Michael Finnissy

afar
   the sea
the eye
   watches…

   grass
at a rock's base
   moves
in thin wind

stretched &
   torn
in precarious
   balance,

   all places
empty to
   Pascal's
space (*m'effraie…*) – the

inkspatter of
   stars, their
inconspicuous traces
   alongside

Alongside

for Michael Finnissy

alongside
       empty mills
and rye-fields,
       riders

       under willows,
by the field's edge
       where rye-stalks stir
in the breeze

small claws
       where leaf-
blade
       meets stem,

       long awns
rising
       from the heads
of the rye

shaken by hooves
       and banners, the
song of bugles,
       afar

walk the line

to walk
far from silently
amid the tumble
of breakers, the
skewed and
varicose roll of
the surf, its
fetch backed up
far beyond the isle's
end and its
thunder ended
in the swirl and hiss
of back-wash back down
through the ochre pebbles:
the sea is not calm
today, but showing
angry white tips
on lip-curling in-
volute trem-
ulous masses of
water cascading:
along the shore
splash and splash
and fall of waves:
this sea trails
a long line of spray,
cradles stone,
steadfast;
embraces, grasps, fondles,
kneads, strokes and polishes
then lets its load drop
onto sluiced
gravel, lack-
ing the vigour

to pull it back
to the ocean,
swash
buckling under
and returning
as back-
wash, waves
moving in each
speck of each
wave…
        from that
grating roar
sound grades
down to where
there's no sound:
ebbing over that
threshold the
white noise
of white water
withdrawing through
shingle, accompan-
iment to the crunch
of cleat on sea-
polished gravel,
laminar pebbles
rememb'ring cliffs
and distant rivers,
moving
slowly
(a)long-shore
drifting: as
force's push
gives in
to gravity's pull
beach-rubble
moves: sorted

assortedly,
each pebble
graded along
the long
littoral…
                under the fall
of a foot's weight
shingle slides
sideways 'til
frictive packing
anchors it: to
walk the line
along the sea's
fringe, on the
shadowed ledge
of the shingle
berm, boot falls
after boot-fall
along the cusp
of the ridge
a brief sun
sits on
under storm–
grey cloud
as heavy as chert,
granite-massy
as the sky
in the storm's
aftermath: salt–
spray vortices
are spun in the air,
spindrift worked
by the endless
wind, droplets ri–
ding in eyebrows
and hair…

                    the clouds
lie low
at the water's edge
behind the shipping
that rode out the weather:
the horizon a line
of thin, pale grey
and the line we're walking
pointillist beige, ovoids of
wave-shaped chert: no
colour else, save the flash
of rich yellow
on a cormorant's
neck...
            fly-catching martins
criss-cross the axis we're tracing
moving into and
out of unison, feet falling
on gravel, repe-
tition repetition,
in cadence as oft-
en as disrup-
ted by chance – and
how is it far, if one
can think of it? – with
grandmotherly care
a skein of wind-
propelled water
wraps itself round
and drenches us all;
new rain spills
from a half
'f a broken boat-
float, gurg
-ling as it percolates
down through the pebbles;

wind bats corks
varec and kelp
across a terrace
of the tide's
making; a piece
of twice-shaped wood
sits stranded, alone,
isolate
from all purpose...
                              light
clarifies
the right-angled
rain-shadow
behind a washed-
up plank, the
ridge is littered with
sea-sculpted plastic
& a moment
of light
hits a
broken oar...
                         brittle
shells, fragile and
hollow, are
scattered, and
gulls' skulls too
dot the shingle,
bleached off-white:
bright compared
to dull gleam of pebbles
water-varnished
but paler under
if turned over to show
bellies ivory as
young herring-gulls'
plumage...

        we're
walking the line,
feeling small pebbles
under our boot-
soles, step after
step after step
after step, pausing only
to lift a curve of float
to find a spider be-
neath it
in a careful, dry, web
replaced with due care
not quite
where it came from…
            leaping

pucker of rain-
pelted water,
squall falling
roughly on beach
and beach-flowers
alike: on sea-
pink, bladed
orache and
sinuous eel-
grass, thin shadows
sparse as
sunlight…
        hic salta,
here sand-grains dance
in the whirling zone
between wave and
sea-floor, obedient to orders
in glossolalic morse
from a rusting hawser
tapping a flagpole…
          stones

guttural under the feet,
small ones weaseling
into each sole's
every crevice
as boots slip
on rolling pebbles: a
cormorant's shadow
is black on grey-
veined water, sea-poppies
as pale as the common
moon, silent, in-
visible, that tugs
at the surf;
ahead, a
new tide, *Silene*
vulgaris, bladder-
weed, riding
on a far slower
swell; sea
-campion's white
globular calices
bright nodes shining
on a ground of buff
gravel, this elongate spine
of fossil diatoms...
                as the in-
step slides pebbles
ride and settle: a
young gull
strokes the water,
the wind
makes waves,
and each wave's
spill, plunge
and surge
renews the beach,

creating, pre-
serving,
destroying;
each sound
lost
in the sound
of water:
though time
might cease,
there's silence here
never;
white froth
climbs, dark waves
break, foam and
tumble
out 'f the loud-
roaring sea,
alongside the scutter
of eddied pebbles
walking their line.

thinking of Evan,
walking on Chesil

the turn, not
linguistic and
not philo-
sophical, but akin
to the swerve 'f a flight
'f plover off shingle,
black backs in fact
as dun as the pebbles
but darkened in shadow,
just 's their fronts 're
whitened by sun
over the diamond sea;
in angles and arcs
moving neither as One
nor as the Many
but in a stochastic weave
pervasive through space,
stiff wing-
beats shape
a loop-
hole in air,
cut through
the hierarchy
of language,
a space where agility
can melt
into sunlight…

Webern sings *The Keel Row* for Howard

voices
singing, tune in
a round,

an air
moving, equal
measure:

turning
the row, held and
dancing –

sae blithe,
sae sprightly an
bonny:

– dancing,
held, a row that's
turning,

measured,
equal, moving
in air;

around
the tune, singing
voices

six translations of Matsuo Bashō's
fūryū-no / hajime ya oku no / ta-ue-uta
inside a poem for Cecilia Vicuña

a beginning,
deep
in labour

as fire
springing,
living –

a start,
poetry
from nowhere:

to find,
now, an
opening,

grace
beginning
in the heart;

seeing,
placed
and busy,

refinement
in the innermost
part –

footprints
mark out
a track,

art
starts
in work –

words
suspended
in air:

aesthetics
initially
song

```
WIND   KEEN
HILL   COLD
FORD   FOUL
LAKE   ICED

SNOW   SKIN
THIN   DEER
HARD   MIRE
RUSH   RIME

COLD   POOL
REED   BARE
HARD   GALE
BARE   TREE

BRAE   PEAK
SNOW   EDGE
HIGH   WIND
BIRD   CALL
```

an egg for E.

ur-
object from
any point of view,
summed mathematical
constraints, ellipsoid in its
flow, both bellied as a viol
and curved like a pear; like
that pair a paradigm of limit:
closed, perfect, pointless,
its point must be its
hatching into the
potentialities
of song

remembering Scott LaFaro

shed notes
leave

    the
double bass

a gentle
heart

  strongly
held

– for who's
absolved

  from
the play

of the
mind?

– wind
and light

move the
leaves

   day
and night

leave no
moves

scored
and cut

my foolish
heart

for August Kleinzahler

Wedding Song

to assay
radiance, speak
or sing:

song falls
as seeds
or spores

and form
is
graceful

for
what else
remains?

– opening
inward, love
remains:

… **speak** …
articulate,
(sing

of)
what
remains:

when ... song
... the mind ...
hearing ...

clear
song ...
beginning –

air
trace
grace

arising
from figures
of speech

– song
of water
and time

illuminating
all
eyes

century's end *ghazal*

frost was, shades were, spectral, grey
whitish washed buff with black speckles

sun weakening
orange-buff, covert

from a woodbine-tangled, exposed-
topped lilac, easily missed, a voice

direct and low, sharp
wind's flight through gloom

frail and thin and gaunt and small
hunger and fear and wind-beruffled

after a short pause
varied, clear-toned, strident

winter's marked repetition
not strictly arranged in verses

over hardly-darkening ling
desolate song

a small *alba*

white the moon
white the wine

white the light
white the leaf

white the rock
white the bark

white the stone
white the dawn

*

pond
the pond
old pond
old-pond
an old pond
the old pond
ancient pond
an ancient pond
the ancient pond
ageing pond
a lonely pond
the quiet pond
frog pond

Afghan *ghazal*

wave of the long grass
as the wind shakes it

small dance of juniper
on the brecciated ridge

on limestone conspicuously abundant
old shells littering the ground

jewel-cases under stones
highly polished and heliciform

on walls   in worm-burrows
in flood-plain exuviæ and silt

plethora of their remnants
hard glossy and polished

pondering foot of steppes
think slow and act slower

ascend in thin light
perfect and complicated

unconsidered but not lost
the connectives not seen

refer to their tiny skyline
distance opens up

o for the principle of hope
in the diaries of these snails

sound shanty for bob cobbing

badcall
balta
eagamoll
eorsa
fara
fidra
fuiary
gigalum
guillamon
huney
lamba
luchruban
mealaster
mullagrach
nibon
noss
oldany
oxna
ristol
samphrey
scarba
soyea
switha
texa
treshnish
tubhard
uyea
uynarey
vementry

Three Misreadings of Horatian Odes

A Misreading of Horace, *Odes* I. 29

your heart on ghazis et acrem militiam
inglorious you stop non before paras
non horribilique as of money
trade aggrandisement and loot

outside ivory gates the economic *burning*
through sponso necato faces of the misery
openly cry on television mani- pulated
parti-coloured or otherwise

will neget arduis carrying sagittas
the tender rivers may see the stars
and stripes keeping totalitarian *swords*
reverti montibus ownership *erect*

you we once thought saner
deaf to the popular flow
'facts' mutare *forsake the Muses*
for shields nobilis *books in dust*

A Misreading of Horace, *Odes* I. 35

Necessity, Goddess who canst, precedes to arms!
O wonder present madder conducted
to our perishable bodies

ingratiating blandishments of office-seekers
you to pauper ambit dominate
preche pretty to our houses

of barbarorum of tyranni
et ferox with hard fierce their head
attributes particularly addressed to the eyes

incapable of distinctness with a careless flick
kick over that marching column
the edifice of society itself vulnerable

the attribution of an abstraction
Necessitas Securitas and *Pax* are leaning on pillars
the sentient polygon "ad weapon"

you white Spes et rare Fides
fraudulent friends   veiled cloth
houses share the suffering

nor quit ne fall / the state's tall
liar an unpoetical word
like dried shit

you serve Caesarem
in we ultimos orbis Britannos
poets cannot have misinterpreted

quid in hard refugimus lasts
venturing on something forbidden
no piety left untouched

o utinam is new facts
hope yet may draw arms
quit *tyranni* blunt with excessive use

A Misreading of Horace, *Odes* IV. 14

quae concern of citizens honorum
afflicted in quotidian affairs

abstraction taken concrete form in troops
nuper quid Marte will not tire

inplacidum foreign nationals et
arces Alpibus milite on high

mox *grave* major (grave)
through rent clouds your duty

speaking to you today ruinis
through language and grammar

at my request south winds scourge
the military capability per ignis

ut barbarorum the perils
horrendamque et war

the conflict et extremo metendo
quo die quo die your country

those sacrifices are laudemque
et optatum massive brutality

imperiis decus this commitment
Medusque missiles on the

te rapidus *Tigris* (Tigris) violence
necessary dominaeque murderers

qui terrorism as an attack
our victory qui remotis.

You have my shaken armis.
The pieces are peaceful nation.

foreign policy (*a performance text*)

History [is] the slaughter-bench at which the happiness of peoples, the wisdom of states and the virtue of individuals have been victimised – Hegel

• We are focussed on Afghanistan. We are making every single effort to avoid civilian casualties. The weaponry that we are using is as targeted as possible. We are very lucky to have the armed services that we do. Nobody was in any doubt. This is a propaganda battle. I mean, you're not dealing with reasonable people; you're not dealing with people you can negotiate with. Our quarrel is not with the ordinary people. • We are focussed on Afghanistan. We are making every single effort to avoid civilian casualties. The weaponry that we are using is as targeted as possible. We are slaughter-bench lucky to have the armed services that we do. Nobody was in any doubt. This is a propaganda slaughter-bench. I mean, slaughter-bench are not dealing with reasonable people; slaughter-bench are not dealing with people slaughter-bench can negotiate with. Our slaughter-bench is not with the ordinary people. • Slaughter-bench are focussed on Afghanistan. Slaughter-bench are making every single effort to avoid civilian casualties. The slaughter-bench that slaughter-bench are using is as targeted as possible. Slaughter-bench are slaughter-bench lucky to have the armed services that slaughter-bench do. Nobody was in any doubt. This is a propaganda slaughter-bench. I mean, slaughter-bench not dealing slaughter-bench reasonable people; slaughter-bench are not dealing slaughter-bench people slaughter-bench can negotiate with. Our slaughter-bench is not with the ordinary people. • Slaughter-bench are slaughter-bench on Afghanistan. Slaughter-bench are slaughter-bench every single effort to avoid civilian casualties. The slaughter-bench that slaughter-bench are using is as targeted as slaughter-bench. Slaughter-bench are slaughter-bench lucky to have the armed services that slaughter-bench do. Nobody was in any doubt. This is a slaughter-bench slaughter-bench. I slaughter-bench, slaughter-bench not dealing slaughter-bench reasonable slaughter-bench; slaughter-bench are not dealing slaughter-bench slaughter-bench slaughter-bench can negotiate with. Our slaughter-bench is not with the ordinary slaughter-bench. • Slaughter-bench are slaughter-bench on Afghanistan. Slaughter-bench are slaughter-bench every slaughter-bench effort to avoid slaughter-bench slaughter-bench. The slaughter-bench that slaughter-bench are slaughter-bench is as targeted as slaughter-bench. Slaughter-bench are slaughter-bench slaughter-bench to slaughter-bench the armed slaughter-bench that slaughter-bench slaughter-bench. Nobody was in any slaughter-bench. This is a slaughter-bench slaughter-bench. I slaughter-bench, slaughter-bench not slaughter-bench slaughter-bench slaughter-bench slaughter-bench slaughter-bench; slaughter-bench are not slaughter-bench slaughter-bench slaughter-bench slaughter-bench slaughter-bench negotiate with. Our slaughter-bench is not with the ordinary slaughter-bench. • Slaughter-bench are slaughter-bench slaughter-bench Afghanistan. Slaughter-bench are slaughter-bench every slaughter-bench effort to slaughter-bench slaughter-bench slaughter-bench. The slaughter-bench that slaughter-bench are slaughter-bench is as slaughter-bench as slaughter-bench. Slaughter-bench are slaughter-bench slaughter-bench to slaughter-bench the armed slaughter-bench that slaughter-bench slaughter-bench. Slaughter-bench was in slaughter-bench slaughter-bench. This is a slaughter-bench slaughter-bench. Slaughter-bench slaughter-bench, slaughter-bench slaughter-bench slaughter-bench slaughter-bench slaughter-bench slaughter-bench; slaughter-bench are slaughter-bench slaughter-bench slaughter-bench slaughter-bench slaughter-bench slaughter-bench slaughter-bench with. Slaughter-bench slaughter-bench is slaughter-bench with the slaughter-bench slaughter-bench. • (*from, and to, Tony Blair*)

white

for Robert Ryman

faded leg
creamy journey
colourless travel
ashen compass
pallid orbit
pearly tour
dull desire
light enduring
gleaming long
lustreless genesis
opalescent spring
candid provenance
immaculate authority
timeless source
creamy ending
snowy rota
anaemic life
pearly finish
pallid clause
colourless period
milky model
lustreless citizen
blanched pattern
ageless paradigm
light subordinate
fading cóntent
shiny subject
bleached pace
creamy tempo
faded gauge
hueless tenor
decoloured cost

pale ratio
pearly rate
bright nexus
achromatic yoke
colourless chain
milky splice
dull detail
anaemic link
niveous moment
leucous time
achromatistous hour
colourless oddity
bright ace
gleaming original
pearly wafer
candid docket
snowy flake
immaculate card
creamy pawn
faded automaton
pale catspaw
opalescent gadget
etiolated chase
candid implement
immaculate tool
clear crust
pallid cortex
ashy chassis
clear jacket
gleaming stone
opaline framework
milky conch
spotless crust
candid superstratum
ashen hull
pearly bomb

lustreless pod
light carapace
bleached shell
immaculate trend
dull fringe
creamy boundary
shiny incline
albescent brink
colourless bend
snowy brim
blanched verge
toneless quorum
colourless quantum
hueless quota
anaemic tip
pallid culmination
unpigmented check
ashen frontier
opaline crown
faded edge
gleaming margin
spotless condition
candid limit
dull diet
pale form
creamy congress
milky enclosure
albescent protocol
snowy summit
shiny synod
pearly law
lactescent convention
clear watch
etiolated chronometer
shiny clock
creamy assemblage

light expedient
pallid assembly
ashen haunt
bright ploy
candid concurrence
achromatic dodge
snowy wile
fading concentration
bleached ruse
anaemic device
pale shift
opalescent artifice
opaline resort
colourless stain
ashy signature
blanched initial
pearly spoil
niveous feature
toneless level
lustreless point
faded cross
gleaming blemish
lactescent scar
ashen prominence
pallid distinction
immaculate smear
spotless blot
unpigmented wrinkle
decoloured scratch
fading reserve
etiolated brand
bleached weal
shiny score
milky pitch
hueless stigma
opaline trait

opalescent tarnish
creamy attribute
albescent welt
pale smudge
anaemic pock
snowy flaw
pallid lineament
light note
bright mark
clear spot

Taliesin

i.m. Ric Caddel

conning difference heart
bright as a pronoun
no false praise singing
truthbread-provider
edging a swift coverlet
you sing page tutor
learn to open a curtain
o vainly coffered stray
offered honeyed singing
at some point aired
call for wine patterned
ardent more than any
sing keening core fact
hateful the seeing
farewell to Caddel
caught light and cogent
son's shade by kirkgate
way work husbanded
and smile late allotted
poured lettered knowledge
spoken technical language
tantamount to birdsong
caught crux superlative
while sound mirrored
words heard collided
not strong but confident
home love near a garden
knack of jewelled movement
in fresh terms braiding
last property overthrown
educate deep internet
familiar translation kernel

yes care for emptied nest
pleasant dust-stook gaffered
endeavour often violet
made ginnelled and ganging
despite chair and committee.
allowed candour conversing
caught in mountain bracken
good yarn rattling
learned truant deserving
cornered rocked and gunning
lyric library visitation
eyesore leviathan leeching
perfect song in the morning
reflecting power lying
rain fall on the igloo
everyone speaking in red
prized byte deck burning
clear light in the kenning

way after the old Welsh of the Canu Taliesin

for Louis Zukofsky, a hundred years on

the
substance

else devoted,
I am shadow

changing thoughts
then this

let me look
on that shadow,

come,
take this

shadow
up,

unseeing
eyes

35 stanzas from *unHealed*

poems in English long after the old Welsh of the *Canu Heledd*

Coalition cannon dappled grey:
They want a thrust though it pierce heads;
toxic chemicals spread over Derah.

Coalition cannon dappled brown:
the gist of language, burning bodies,
they have taken Derah, a desolate town.

Coalition shelling over the boundary:
chain-guns, *co-ax*, the armies
captured Derah, a town with no fathers.

Coalition rifles open fire:
chain-guns, *hesh*, the soldiers
captured Derah, no-one left alive.

Coalition cannon moving haphazardly
into the tumult of battle,
cannon, cannonade, carnage.

•

Nothing mollifies tonight,
outside on hard rock.
No-one, no people.

Dark and sad tonight –
no fire and no books.
Tears erode the cheeks.

Dark and sad, tonight –
no fire, no household.
Crying at nightfall.

It breaks me to see –
no shelter, no fire.
Pools of destruction.

Desolate tonight;
after the soldiers,
faces are altered.

.

eagle *erne* 'golden' **tonight**
white-tailed glides grouped **bespattered**
eye whirling trees **longing** yearly

eagle 'f **el-Huir** all gleaming higher
bloodstained young nests boreal
eye whirling trees hunt **grief**

eagle *erne* **oppressive** hunting
different mid-air **tonight**
dark brownish **long** rain gliding

eagle *erne* estuaries **seas**
name threat plumage in eaglet
game-birds **sees** old woods grey

eagle *erne* **flies** cliffs hunting
carrion eyes **feasting**
all larger lighter heads' **violence**

.

The driftpin finds a *dinar*
it hefts, yells – victor.
The quiet of dawn drifts in gear.

The driftpin isn't different –
law and order not worth a gourmand's cat.
The garrison nigh dying.

The driftpin drank, drained the throat white.
Oud, gnawed, aches, urgent, torn. In debit the gut
each noon-tide echoed.

.

Moving in parallel the Euphrates
and by trenches the Tigris
and there are torsoes in the Khabur.

Moving in parallel the two rivers Zab
and by ditches the Diyala
and there's gore in the Uzaym.

.

watcher wearied in tabu ringed
a herd bend in hate
grown wrong chant

watcher wearied in tabu ringed
a chant be in retch
grown wrong duty

wrath gadgetry threw way edgy
a wrath eddy a wind ode
wage idly war

.

Law views better are vital,
conquest, coalition, campaign,
is assure true, troops destruction.

No shadow wealth are new coalition:
not through deliver with.
No vital a free fear look.

Better aim benefit any falls,
a develops forces while oil.
Of from an event oil.

Better am benefit a too do regime.
Vital aim forward access get.
Nor government falls *yr ffuc*.

•

Sargon   Hammurabi   Cyrus   Antiochus
Hormizd   Harun al-Rashid   Faisal
the Administrators of the Coalition Provisional Authority

•

Amputation blackened flies fire.
Parts blast shards heads crowd.
Gutted metal smoking toppled blast stump.

Amputation blackened flies fire.
Parts blast shards limbs wounded.
Gutted metal smoking toppled shrapnel.

Amputation blackened flies fire. Blackened
flies flames legs wreckage.
Guts blast smoke toppling congealed.

•

fully field programmable
with in-flight re-targeting
to cover the whole kill chain

with sensor-to-shooter capability
for effects-based engagement
and an integral good-faith report

and a situational awareness
of integrity and trust
to achieve the desired lethal effects

•

Misan	Block 4	Majnoon	Block 9
Khabbaz	Rafidan	Rumaila	Jambur
Luhais	Safwan	Safiya	Qurna

•

•

•

Processions written inside chivalry

Even as bush, odd as
    light
For how long can they be an
    extravagance beyond their regular call?

A kind of people
This sleep bears no relation to
    chart, east, heart, angel

There is that procession like the
    heat driving the windows

Here is a bird, a
    home, a prison, storms for an assault
They are sunny and
    scornful of anything that is
      victorious
Plumed as time,
    torrid as town
"I know wizard-fingers",
    they cry, until they
      are naked
Want a trifle

They have no air
Here there are
    convictions
Such esteem bears no
    relation to loss, extremity, creature, tree

"Harry Gilonis"

Blair's Grave

Opening The Grave, a poem bid
to paint air to judgement
Blake's television yonder
Horrid apparition   British prime
amidst skulls screened
in mild repose depicted
the renovated social man
wreaked order

                            rich and visible
with lies as appointed
the science of being wrong
superficial but deep
Blair outreach'd wandered heedless on
Soul exhilarated by leadership
he happily Britain
Quite by glory task
intoxicated by dreams eternal
theologians hovering
with harps   under arms
issues of trust or integrity over
intelligence was remotely
Peace mistakes have been made
everyone is happy hugely
the virtuous own the banks
thrones and chemicals

.

errors were made on our side and face
sword happen'd
the wrong weapons traded into the hands
good war more happily our good
my fervent global threat
screened to confusion   air to shreds
the world over
preparing for futures

•

Newsnight insignia mended his song
I never anticipated spending time on irony
let's be clear once this row dies
I don't do Hell
slime made of men
others' the abyss   the horror   not mine
Blood thick   sooty gross
the war on right thing
never us
heaving righteousness becalmed
gross   slow   moving
"we strove hard for the strong"

•

past buried country
banners   folly   disastrous
Black cloud   the moral air
ethical cleansing
logistical nightmare democracies
privatise the doing
Fedex the coffins
pile dead pride
immortality is up
exploring futures doleful black

·

the eglantine smell'd of science
blossoms hampering the shipment of food
the virtuous own the banks
thrones and chemicals
dark as war
                ragged English legacy
made of epitaphs
riding beneath the crows
to meet nothing but flame
sword in the shiver, on the hid
How calm his exit!

·

from *NORTH HILLS*

'faithless' translations of classical Chinese poetry
(presented here in paired versions)

quite a way after Li Shang-yin (AD 813–858)

inlaid harp

patterned zither not carry five ten strings
one string one fret consider magnificent years
Chuang Tzu day dream confused butterfly butterfly
Wang Emperor youthful heart entrust restrict cuckoo
green sea moon bright beads are tears
blue field sun warm white grow smoke
this situation able stay become pursue remember
merely is being when stop desolate thus

bright strings

bright strings handled
gut, peg...   thought
bewilderment   flutters by
night jars   transformed
clear understanding
on an indigo field
a problem pursued
at the time   right

quite a way after Po Chü-I (AD 772–846)

as grass

leaves leaves prairie grasses
here once   gone once
fire consumes fire weed
head-high in spring-wind
fragrant invasion by roads
bright extension by walls
prince of friends leaving / luxuriant
'flamingo feathers' waving him off...

grasses primer

grasses leave, leave barren plains
in a year flourish, within it wither
tundra fires never quite burn grass off
new spring brings new life to meadows
smell of green crosses the old road
sight of green enters the old town
when my old friend Timothy leaves
I'm bent, I'm lorn, I'm down – it's hard...

quite a way after Tai Shu-lun (AD 732–789)

old friend

autumn pours us full
night levels towns cities
chanced meeting   beyond geography
flitting about time time
wind moves magpie / words
Spider-web flutters clear night
travellers with wine constant
kept mutual in looped days

old friend

fall moon fills us
in night-doubled cities
balanced accounts   within histories
translating doubts   every time
dark winds   measured words
insects crawl // in the white-out
travellers with wine constant
kept mutual   at azimuth

quite a way after T'ao Ch'ien (c. AD *365–427*)

drinking wine [*no. 5 of a sequence*]

home amid great works
noise of communication traffic
ask about paying cash
breakdown of partial sincerity
(doesn't match any documents)
mountain walking genre poem
beautiful painless night signals
rhythmic propulsion birds roost
work   progress   meaning mystifying
link posts   neglect speech

drinking wine [*no. 5 of a sequence*]

a house shaped   near folk, but not too near
no noise of traffic on the roadways
how so? how so? how? so.
mind & heart   distanced   self inclines to place
see: fuchsia fuchsias interlace the hedgerows
Galtymore a line of thin pale russet
(the beauty of mountain air at dusk)
birds move to roost together:
this. here. true. clear. meaning?
(distant) *petalled by memory* (echo)

quite a way after Ts'ui Hao (AD 704–754)

brown crane

a yellow crane   left
yellow crane tower   right
looked for in vain
… centuries of clouds …
clear sky streams trees
through the plain of grasses
day(s) end(s) going home
mist / waves / river

crane (version)

1. lifted by crane to heaven
2. subordinated earth left empty
3 (not) repeated (not) duplicated
4. sky loaded with clouds (folded thousands)
5. river, trees, positively bright (experience, experience)
6. plumed birds, grasses (luxuriant, luxuriant)
7. sunset uncertainty (where are the bureaucrats?)
8. roll-up smoke signals across the water

quite a way after Ts'ui Shu (c. AD 704–749)

elevated station

how imperious this vantage
from which to assess the day
cloud peeks at each cardinal point
the news is 'rain' from along the valley
closing the passes off from view
here among old banks and slaughter-houses
how unexpected to find poets
and enthusiasts for chrysanths and antiques

nine clouds

high masts of the imperium
watch the weather becoming dawn
anvil clouds heading north
…rain in from Yosemite…
One never knows, do one?
whirling matters dervish-style
leave it to poets *o nombreux officiers*
to ruminate cloud-types and flowers

quite a way after Tu Fu (AD 712–770)

moonlight night

tonight   under foreign moon
the room   watches   alone
distant   pity   tiny   few
can't explain   won't remember
hair fragrant cloud(-top)
clear   pure   bright   armed
what   when   relied on
ears dried   brightness shared

night moon

exiled moon tonight
she watches alone
far family sorrow
remembering not here
sweet cloud hair missed
clear light flesh called
empty casement time
tears dried together

*quite a way after Tu Mu (*c. AD 803–852*)*

southern spring

calling / birds / reflect (off/on) river
water, village, mountain, ramparts, flags, wind…
many, many (many many) temples
pavilions (in) mist (in) rain

southern spring

foliage, blossom, orioles
mountains and rivers and pubs and banners
facing south, morning
architecture & unfrozen rain

*quite a way after 'Tzü Yeh' (*fl. AD 3rd–4th centuries*)*

attributed song 1.0

long night   no sleep
moon shine bright bright
thought I heard   quiet voice
said "you" to no-one, no-where

attributed song 1.1

night blank   particles of sleep
moon embeds brilliance redoubled
voice blankly scatters
emptiness   affirmatively

quite a way after Wang Wei (c. AD 700–760)

deer park   (*poem 5 from* Wheel River)

no change on the hollow hills
sole solo voice duplicated
flickering light through trees
falls on blue lichen

deer enclosure   (*poem 5 from* Wheel River)

wild sky | HILLS | unseeing people
still   conversation sounding
brightness moves into deep woods
again shines again onto green moss

quite a way after Wei Chuang (AD 836–910)

pictured landscape

rain   fall   falls   river
birds move   empty air
deluged in willows
(in) hidden (cigarette-smoke) mist

Jinling landscape

rain shadows rain   falls falls   lateral stalks
quantitative as-if dream: larks sang (air)
suspended   *fair field*   within
riuer narrows   walls of a city   borrowed light

quite a way after Yu Hsüan-chi (AD 844–869)

poem responding

the crowds the people the noise the glare
quietly sitting   set apart
not looking for company nor even an elegant phrase
finding a *mot juste* in a moated village
for your simple flowers   I'm grateful
rusticated, learning my -ologies
so full of affection that I need no-one
one living in mountains … pines

poem responding (remix)

flung amid an accident of noise
silence banishes mandolins
work a jewel bound on my finger
distilling the propounded word
clematis – denotes – result
held – aloof – to learn
symptoms of affection   perception
pine   heedless fellow of mountains

quite a way after Ch'ien Ch'i (AD 722–780)

abandoned person

two yellow birds through woods
overcast (at dawn) overcast
flower bells exhausted
rain among water-willows
warm sun specific
cherished (with both hands)
poems still not wanted
hair white, face & future blank

gift accepted

bright birds blur woodland
shady city outskirts
flower-clocks sounding patterns
willows parting long water
electric roadways divide
elder blossom held in mind
poems met with offers
such readiness / magnificent

quite a way after Li Po (AD 701–762)

wasted visit

dog sound   water bark
rain   heavy   blossoms
trees deep with deer
beck hears no bell
bamboo split mist
water hangs from peaks
where is 'here' no-one knows
pine on pine on

no way

((water)) (dog) within (bark) ((sound))
peach blossoms distil the dew
deer // deep woods // appear
above   the stream   [   ] unheard
((blue)) (bamboo) divides (bamboo) ((mist))
springs   wing from green cliffs
not-to-have / not-to-know / just   to go
still   weary   pines   twice, thrice

quite a way after Li Shang-yin (AD 813–858), again

no title

exquisite zither's fifteen strings
fretfully bridge time lost & spent
(butterfly dreams shivering scales,
cuckold-cuckoo sings in spring;
these pearls that were moons tears
from a long way off, smoky-grey)
how hold lost time immaterial
gone in a flash amidst bewilderment

That harp…

That harp – sounds – feathering the air
fretting / trembling / the flowery mountain
racket for the contemporary moment
springs amorous ('…pretty… …warbles…') blurred
travelling blues going in your direction
step into not knowing "the summits again"
with a feeling cadences ring through memory
merely spatio-temporal, perplexed and lost

an epithalamy, or ballad

love is put to the test – Wittgenstein

calm the day, and bright;
constructed space and time
altering surroundings;

below skies
water-encircled
in the lee of the land,

larks sang matutinal
in sunlit air, that mote
your mind delight…

– ordered nature
transfigures itself
to ordered world –

a place and a purpose
intangible but simple,
long-looked-for joy…

now is it time
commitment calling
through scatterd light,

love manifest
ut tenax hedera
arborem implicat

now is time unfolding,
minute accumulations
in the texture of air:

– such knowledge fragmentary
until unconcealment,
minutes accumulating…

a purpose and a place
for solace and happiness: truth
is there too, in calm and quiet

paired magpies fly;
light through cloud, then
wind through reeds –

all things established
in graceful dance
where rest and peace are found,

glad affection
deliberate and resolved
through sweet consent:

may suns strengthen
and winds caress:
we're wishing good luck in all things.

Bass adds Bass

for Dom Lash and his bass

Bass adds
bass, wrap-
-ping round
a line,

taking
it for
a walk:

stand-
-up
　　up-
right

holding im-
-mediacy,
no abstract
nothing

a dis-
-ruption
into
form,
　　force
expend-
-ed to
an end

strong, ac-
-tive and
voracious

charac-
-terised by
abun-
dance and
excess,

dance of
power
and weight,
a firm
& fast
footing

and harm-
-onious
devel-
-opment

hand o-
-ver hand

so *add a*
little bass,
a low wave
become audible

under
the song,
deter-
-minedly
indeter-
-minate
:

mechanisms
of affinity
closely
modelled

...brushed, dragged
and smeared, simul-
-taneously tangled;
scraped, wiped
and scratched...

bringing objects
before the mind
in de-
-finite thought:

change the
phrase, change
the *phase*

the process ac-
-centuated;
                        – whence
the bass, nearly
black, dark & impure –

brim-full of content,
translated to
immediacy

(a soft boom,
a hoarse roar)

suspended
in difference,

indifference
suspended:

setting the
rhythm,
minute,
particular

pure apper-
-ception
looking out
for the beat

the straight
line and
the curve

knotted and
projecting

capacity
& power,

practical
builder of
elegant
convergences:

the sound
brightens
time and
possibility,

abstract,
unfettered:

in the beginning
what was there?
in the first place,
start from being

the end not
identical with
the object

thus, after
the beat,
thrum and pulse:

it's a ba–
ba–
ba–
ba–
ba–
bass –

Georg Trakl fails to write a Christmas poem

white sky. black jackdaws. grey forest.
white treetops. black sky. grey jackdaws.
white forest. black treetops. grey sky.
white jackdaws. black forest. grey treetops.

.

red branches.
red snowfall.
red nights.
red darkness.

.

purple snow, purple wine.
purple midnight. purple wine.

blue snow, blue wine.
blue midnight. blue wine.

silver snow, silver wine.
silver midnight. silver wine.

David Davis's bone density

beyond the startling
calyx of teeth
[...] asylum   (Trevor Joyce)

wanting to see
genuine children
brought in

carried along
on a tide
of emotion

a well-grown 2-year-old
may be mistaken
for older

formerly judgemental
of physical appearance
and demeanour

people need to have
confidence in moving
to dental checks

milking it
temporary replaced
by permanent

teeth at the
corners of this 4-
year-old mouth

influenced by
nutrition and
the environment

past their peak
when 9 to 10
years of age

we need to be quite
hard-nosed here
people are desperate

there is a
terrible intelligence
working inside

the mouth
opened by
powerful hands

eyes expressionless
with tears in
mesh-link fencing

callous
written
on the heart

the scream continues
builds
abruptly stops

a spokesman said
we can't satisfy
what you want

knowledge
and informed
consent

is it safe
is it safe
is it safe

inappropriate and
unethical when
of no benefits

The Matter of Ireland

for Billy Mills

Turquoise
Hornblende
Epidote

Pitchstone
Rhodonite
Obsidian
Pyroxene
Erinite
Rutile
Topaz
Iron
Epistilbite
Sapphire

Olivine
Felspar

Selenite
Tin
Onyx
Nickel
Emerald

Revisions (after Roy Fisher)

ut varias usus meditando extunderet artia (Georgics 1.133)

Virgil
taking hours over it   losing them
into a poised gleam
a single light

•

Coping Batter

for Tom Raworth

chip and block
cleavage footing
bed chain
wedge runner
head joint
face jumper
crown grit
tie spar
flag course
stoop through
rag pinnings
buck and doe

a breath of air
branches like trees,
lighting
small increments of change;
heard sound
climbs
as song ramifies,
and, speaking, *sees*:
part
and apart,
as music strives,
doing, saying
finely
by hand, for us –
ranging, now, high to low,
patterns dying
that don't give satisfaction.

they were so clear,
those first strophes,
stating
how heart, ears, interchange,
move round:
time's
sequence codifies
all theories,
art
and non-art;
jouissance contrived
for those hearing
truly –
accretive, plus
evolving, fast or slow –
moments passing,
distilled out of abstraction.

to be prepared
and *know the keys*,
finding
broken airs (tunes) exchanged;
such ground
rhymes
feedback [specialised]
and syntheses
(thought
and un-thought);
hands re-derive
right-brain thinking
clearly –
monoceros
(no rustic *chalumeau*)
embodying
motor-movements' exaction.

the song can dare
these clarities,
shaping
as modulations range:
compound
chimes
materialise
lancets, in threes,
arch
on curved arch;
high-pitched, roof dives
(red-tiled ceiling):
roundly-
drawn lines move, thus,
describe a circle, so:
curves, relieving –
part of delight's attraction.

unfolding spare
polyphonies
shifting
overtones re-arrange,
expound:
mind
that's active denies
minds from bodies
part
– they can't part,
not while alive! –
such conjoining
wholly
analogous,
moving *gemutató*
(demonstrating)
de motu, 'about motion'.

from otherwhere
rare densities
making
the familiar strange,
new-found:
lines
cross, don't cross, surprise
by strategies;
heart
sings *by heart*
how joy shapes lives –
music, feeling
singly
brilliant corners –
no frowns as flurries flow,
snake, deciding
it's 'instant composition'.

accord connives
(*remir*) seeing:
plainly
it's marvellous,
hurtling *prestissimo* –
endings're endings –
scarce time for introspection.

Acknowledgements & Annotations

'And the light falls, *remir*' – Ezra Pound

Ever since Pound put the word *remir* (Provençal, 'I gaze') into his Canto xx, trusting the reader to unpack the reference (a highly-charged moment in a poem by Arnaut Daniel), it has been a risky, but licit, gambit in poetry to condense allusion as well as diction. (Basil Bunting told Pound he'd once encountered a German-Italian Dictionary that embedded the concept in a definition: '*Dichten*: *condensare*'.) There is, below, some information relevant to such unpacking of my poems herein. I've tried to leave it at that; as Charles Olson reminded Jonathan Williams, 'a poem is a process, not a memoir'. The intent, then, is not to 'explain': as Bunting said, the reader is as clever as the poet, and, indeed, is also the co-maker of any reading. The poems are *themselves*, and would be so without any annotations. But why not be easy and democratic about such things?

The poems appear in approximately chronological order, with some minor adjustments that made for a better grouping or pace. I have excluded from this book those of my translations where a conventional model of fidelity is intended (as, e.g., *For British Workers: Versions of Vladimir Mayakovsky and others* (London: Barque Press, 2017). An asterisk at the head of an entry below indicates that the poem is previously unpublished.

*   *   *

Catullus played Bach first appeared in *Oasis* magazine (1990) and in Richard Caddel's '26 New British Poets' supplement to *New American Writing* magazine (1991). The opening reverses a phrase in Louis Zukofsky's long, Bach-obsessed poem *"A"*: 'Bach read Catullus'. An aria from Bach's *Matthew Passion*, 'Erbarme dich…', contains the phrase *schaue hier*, 'look thou hither'; it has a famous *obbligato* violin part. There are some snippets from Leopold Mozart's still-used treatise on violin-playing, found on my father's bookshelves; *arco* is the musical Italian term for '[played with the] bow'. *Prati ultimi flos* is from Catullus, poem xi: 'at the meadow's edge a flower'.

* **a song-sing** is for the poet, editor, publisher and critic Peter Quartermain; it elaborates on Stephen Dedalus peeing on Sandymount Strand.

* **[For Tony Baker]** is for the poet, also editor/publisher of the important little magazine *Figs*. Richard Feynman is the American quantum physicist, an enthusiasm of Tony's at the time. *Fall* is (Wittgensteinian) German for whatever-is-the-case, as well as American autumn.

* The *cover versions* are just that: William Carlos Williams's 1934 poem 'This is just to say…' put through an antique online translation engine, and then that process reversed. The (mis-)readings generated must (logically) relate to features of their 'source' languages, offering qualities and charms that a non-native speaker could not have 'written'. An October 2017 Catalan cover here replaces an earlier Spanish one.

* **Songbook** was an abortive project to produce translations as *distant* from their (ancient Chinese) originals – poems in the *Shih Ching* ['Book of Songs'] – as possible; a notion spawned by the fact of the immense polyvalency of most ideograms in *Mathews' Chinese-English Dictionary*.

* The line **from a Hebridean notebook** was written whilst in the Outer Hebrides, walking along the fringes of the *machair*, a unique and fragile ecosystem: the meeting-point of alkaline shell-sand and acidic peat makes for a well-drained, neutral soil that, in spring, hosts an astonishing flora – and many rabbits.

* The **two carnivore sonnets** refer to two dragonflies found in the UK, the ruddy darter and the golden-ringed dragonfly.

* The 5 **Latin poems** comprise 'English' homonyms found in the Latin text of poems from Horace's Fourth Book of *Odes*; a gentle exploration of the friendships involved in the *faux ami*. My work can seem to divide between an early quasi-Objectivist mode in which the poem reflects a 'truth' about the 'world', followed later by a 'linguistic turn'. These early poems, from the mid-'80s, spoil that neat account.

there is from every thing… first appeared in *Figs* magazine (1987). Llyn Peris is a lake in a glacial valley near Llanberis, in north Wales. Two phrases come from Salvatore Quasimodo's 'Isola di Ulisse' (*risonanze effimere*; *acqua stellata*). When this was written, I didn't know Bunting's *Briggflatts*, so the half-echo of 'Orion strides over Farne' is accidental. The Welsh phrase (mine, not from any canonical source) describes the scene: 'clear sky and clear night'.

Daruma first appeared in my *Louis Zukofsky, or Whoever Someone Else Thought He Was* (Twickenham and Wakefield: North and South, 1988) - see Zukofsky's 1961 poem of the same title. A *daruma* is a Japanese good luck mascot in the shape of a squat figurine. Initially both its eyes are blank matt-white ovals, and my poem describes its correct subsequent handling.

remembering Paul Haines first appeared in *Other Poetry* magazine (1988), and honours the Canadian poet and librettist for Carla Bley; his words for her 1974 album *Tropic Appetites* supply the closing couplet.

The **Five Impromptus** first appeared in my first book of poems, *Reliefs* (Dublin: hardPressed Poetry, 1988; reprinted Durham: Pig Press, 1990). *Zettel* (German, 'scrap of paper') is the editorial title given to a posthumous collation of such from the copious leavings of Ludwig Wittgenstein. The 199th 'scrap' reads, 'Suppose someone were to say "imagine this butterfly exactly as it is, but ugly instead of beautiful?!".'

liquid (Cona... first appeared in *Figs* magazine (1987), and was reprinted in *Reliefs*. I don't suppose many can still remember Cona coffee machines, which made indifferent coffee rather noisily.

The **Two Poems from the English of the Wordsworths** first appeared in *Reliefs*; see further Philip Terry's Introduction to this book.

for Lorine Niedecker honours the undervalued American poet; it first appeared in *Reliefs*.

start / with what / you know... is also from *Reliefs*. It uses a song-lyric of Tim Hodgkinson in which those who presume to speak for a crowd to which they don't belong so 'betray once more the people who get made into crowds'. George Oppen, as throughout, is behind any mention of 'clarity', here from *Of Being Numerous* 22: 'Clarity // In the sense of *transparence*, / I don't mean that much can be explained.' Oppen's earlier poem 'Antique' speaks of 'survival's / thin, thin radiance'. See also Aristotle's *Metaphysics* (Book v, 1017b): '"Being" and "that which is" mean that some [...] things [...] "are" potentially, others in complete reality [...] we say the Hermes is in the stone, and the half of the line is in the line, and we say of that which is not yet ripe that it is wheat'.

to catch / the 'grain' / of things..., also from *Reliefs*, draws on walks with poets: Tony Baker in the Derbyshire White Peak, and Jonathan Williams along the banks of the Rawthey. Wood melick (*Melica uniflora*) is a delicate and beautiful grass.

Song for Annie is also from *Reliefs*. A 'clew' (or 'clue') is a ball of thread, often assembled from small pieces; one was used by Theseus to escape from the labyrinth, and the word has been used figuratively for solutions to perplexities or difficulties. The quotation is from Elizabeth Barrett Browning's *Aurora Leigh*.

The six **Axioms** were completed in 1989; I first appeared in *Oasis* magazine (1990), II in *Grille* magazine (1992) and IV and VI in *screens and tasted parallels* magazine (1990). The full set was published as a book co-authored with David Connearn, who made a series of intercalary drawings (Cambridge: Ankle Press, 1994; reprinted, 1998). David has made two new drawings specifically for this book. The poems 'read' the solo soprano saxophone playing of Steve Lacy (on two Italian live LPs called *Axieme*) *through* Ludwig Wittgenstein's posthumously-published *Remarks on the Foundations of Mathematics*; music and words share a concern for testing things out for their truthfulness. There are some small-scale textual borrowings from poems by Rainer Maria Rilke and David Miller (to whom the first two sections are dedicated), song lyrics by Peter Blegvad (dedicatee of IV), and the sleeve-notes to Hugh Hopper's masterpiece, *1984* (1973), by John Agam, dedicatee of the final section. Section II refers specifically to Lacy's composition 'The New Duck'.

on the white / grass… first appeared in *Other Poetry* magazine, issue 25 (1989).

Theory first appeared in *Stride* magazine (1989); the examples of phenomena not easily mapped by traditional mathematical physics are from René Thom (quoted in Woodcock & Davis's 1978 *Catastrophe Theory*).

* The **lines for David Bellingham** (photographer, artist, writer and publisher) permute the photographer Ilse Bing: 'Repetition, even at the highest level of craftsmanship, is empty, therefore: SAY IT ONCE!'. David and I share a taste for the music of The Fall; an early 7″ single has it that the 3 'R's are 'repetition, repetition and… repetition'.

Descant on a Theme by Brian Coffey first appeared in *Other Poetry* magazine (1990). I suspect Coffey first met the *ch'ien* [鶼] bird in Apollinaire's *Zone*, where it is called a *pihi*; I have not been able to trace it in Su Tung-p'o (a favourite poet of Coffey). *Suspendat hirundo*, 'the swallow hangs down', is a piece of close observation of the bird's roosting habits from Virgil's *Georgics* (IV.307). 'All the summer long is the swallow a most instructive pattern of unwearied industry and affection', writes Gilbert White in the *Natural History of Selborne* (1789). *Elth', elthe, chelidon*, [ηλθ' ηλθε χελιδών], 'comes, comes the swallow', is the Greek poet Theognis's song of their arrival. Pliny the Elder says swallows do not go far when they migrate, but 'only to sunny valleys in the mountains' (*Naturalis Historia*, x); the poem's close gives Gilbert White's different, and decidedly odd, take on the hibernatory behaviour of swallows in Hampshire – from <u>his</u> *Natural History*.

from far away is a 'hyakuin' or 100-stanza *renga* (a Japanese linked-verse form); it was co-written with the poet Tony Baker, then living 'far away' from me in rural Derbyshire, as I from him in London. I wrote the first, and all subsequent odd-numbered stanzas; he the second, and all subsequent even-numbered ones. The opening of the sequence was published as a stand-alone letterpress broadside, *renga* (Vancouver, BC: Slug Press, 1990); two further extracts appeared in *screens and tasted parallels* magazine, and the whole sequence in *West Coast Line* magazine (both 1990) and as a co-authored stand-alone book (London: Oasis Books, 1998). The 'post / script' to the Oasis edition proffers some of the 'less evident sources of these noises' in the canonical order of the subject-categories of *renga*:

'persons beasts and insects': autumn crocus 7 (line 2 – see Geoffrey Grigson's *Englishman's Flora*); blackberries 46, 47; the northern English (and Scottish) flower *Campanula rotundifolia* 99; spring sandwort/'leadwort' (*Minuartia verna*), locally rife in the lead-mining areas of Derbyshire 9; the mushroom *Geastrum triplex* 30; and Fern – a poet's cat – 1.

'signs of persons': *writers*, Aristotle 47; Walter Benjamin 75; the Bible 31; William Blake (rough draft) 87; Basil Bunting 45, 95; Paul Celan 97; A.H. Clough 77; the Confucian classics 81; Dashiell Hammett 51; Heidegger 69; Krazy Kat (G. Herriman) 31; Jorge Manrique 33; Pound 43 (his funeral, in Venice), 44, 61; Proust 21; Arthur (and Evgenia) Ransome – their joint grave 99; 'Uncle Remus' (J.W. Riley) 47; William Carlos Williams (last letter to James Laughlin) 41; Parson James Woodforde (via Jane Grigson) 81; Louis Zukofsky 35 – *musicians*, anonymous folk 5, 21; Scots piping 52, 53; Captain Beefheart 47; Cage 28; Debussy 5; Delius 19; Ives 13, 67, 90; Thelonius Monk 95; – and *artists*, Joseph Beuys 68, 85; Hans Hofmann 67; R.B. Kitaj 83; Stanley Spencer (his decorations in Burghclere chapel, near the Greenham Common air-base) 59.

'peaks' and other places 'travelled to' (or lived in): Derbyshire 2, 48, 49 (an old lead-miners' pub in Winster), 64, 70, 90; the Lake District 99; Lakeland rivers 3 (Ure and Eden); Northumberland 63, 69; Wales 74, 75 (Porth Neigwl); the Yorkshire Dales 62, 69.

'grievances': Greenham Common 59; the greed of landlords – Marx, footnoting J.S. Mill, on kelp cultivation in the Hebrides – 39; the sub-languages of advertising (23, 40) and politics (11, 30, 42, 84); oil pollution 51, 52; the hubris of 'authoritative sources' 47 (Aristotle's text is properly Latinised as *insecutabilibus*, 'indivisible'), 61.

Not least there are words about love; which must speak for itself, or remain silent.

The Matter of Britain was published as a year's-end postcard (1990); the title is a term for the corpus of mediaeval stories surrounding King Arthur. Here it is taken more literally, as a 'materialist' acrostic is generated from 'matter', from the names of British minerals. This isn't a 'pure' process (unlike, say, some of Jackson Mac Low's work), as there is a considerable element of choice involved; trying to keep metrical and sonorous variety, avoid the same endings too many times in a row, *et cetera*. Indeed, I didn't initially pay close enough attention; it was only when assembling this book that I realised how inappropriate the original line 4, 'Dolomite', was; found in the UK, yes, but obviously far more closely associated with Italy.

The **Win(s)ter Songs** were published in a special 'Pastoral' issue of *fragmente* magazine (1991). Winster is the Derbyshire village where the poet Tony Baker used to live; the poems, however, have a more complex history than 'records of country walks'. Peter Riley's *Strange Family* (Providence, RI: Burning Deck, 1973), declared itself on first publication to be a 'Missa Parodia super Lucis Diei Cantiones Jeremiae Prinni'. My 'Songs' draw on both *Strange Family* and on *Day Light Songs* (Pampisford, Cambs and Cheltenham, Glos: R. Books, 1968).

The **three** *haiku* were first published in *Haiku Quarterly* (1991) and their haikuesque **relation** in Kirkup, Cobb, and Mortimer's *The Haiku Hundred* (Cullercoats, North Shields: Iron Press, 1992, reprinted 2015).

content fitting form first appeared as the first of many Form Books form-Cards, for the year's-end in 1992; a riposte by Brian Coffey was published as card no. 2, and the two pieces together appeared in Coffey's final book, *salute/verse/circumstance* (London: Form Books, 1994, reprinted 2005).

Learning the Warblers was published as a book (London: Writers Forum, 1993). The texts are a response to a set of decidedly conventional poems on bird-watching by the sound- (and page-) poet P.C. Fencott; they are collaged from a wide range of bird-books to produce the sound-poems Fencott *might* have come up with. I briefly re-ordered the set to follow the now-standard British Ornithologists' Union listing order, but didn't like the results, aesthetically, and have here kept to the original order, that of Peterson, Mountfort and Hollom's once-canonical field-guide. There can be limits to the rigorousness of process.

The **Horatian Ingredients** were first published as a pair of postcards (1993). The bi-millennial anniversary of the Roman poet Horace in 1992 prompted my anthology *Horace Whom I Hated So* (London: Five Eyes of Wiwaxia); remembering Erica Van Horn and Simon Cutts's garlic-heavy collaboration *Aglio 6 Olio* (Docking, Norfolk: Coracle, 1992), I asked her to 'illustrate' Horace's garlic-phobic 3rd *Epode* therein. The poetry librarian Geoffrey Soar, hearing of the proposed anthology, gave me a couple of laurel (bay) leaves from Horace's villa, visited by him and his wife Val; they were reproduced on the cover of the finished book.

A *ghazal* is an Arabic-Persian verse-form made up of couplets connected by mood rather than narrative. My **northern** *ghazal* (published as an end-of-year card in 1993) ends, as such poems formally should, with a 'pen-name'; not that of its author, but one given to 'Wavy Hair-grass', a tenacious, sturdy grass usually indicative of poor-quality moorland soils. Bunting's *Briggflatts* presents, persuasively, the idea that animals and plants are reasonable *dramatis personae* for a poem, on an equal standing with humans and not to be idly anthropomorphised.

The **forty fungi** (Docking, Norfolk: Coracle, 1994; reprinted online by *onedit* at www.onedit.net/issue9/harryg/harryg001.html (1997) and as a physical book a year later (Ballybeg, Co. Tipperary, Éire: Coracle, 2008)) are forty poems of forty syllables each, dealing with forty wild mushrooms found in the UK, all with English 'common names', all met by me in the field, and – where known to be edible – eaten by me. Each mushroom is illustrated by the book's co-author, Erica Van Horn.

field mushroom (for Lesley Simms): encountered on a visit to the Simmses near Bellingham in Northumberland; nearby Hesleyside gives its name to the gorgeous Northumbrian small-pipe tune 'Sweet Hesleyside'.

penny bun (for Simon Cutts, a great poet of foodstuffs): *B. edulis* is the cep or porcini of chefs; the circular, sticky cap resembles the old-fashioned 'sticky bun'. 'Mycorrhizal', technical term for a mushroom/plant co-dependency, often crucial to both species. The first 'pattern-poem' in this book.

chanterelle (for Arthur Haswell): an apricot-coloured mushroom found walking with him near the South Tyne in Northumberland.

velvet shank (for Colin Simms, poet-naturalist): Watch Crags, above the Chirdon Burn near Bellingham in Northumberland.

orange birch bolete (for the late Kathleen Cooper, who introduced me to mycology).

blewit (for Alec Finlay, *haiku* and *renga* enthusiast): the italicised poem is after a *haiku* by Bashō (it opens 'matsutake ya', identifying Bashō's mushroom as the 'pine mushroom', *Tricholoma matsutake*). Blewits used to be sold in markets in Derbyshire, called there 'blue-legs' (their stems – *stipes* – being a blue-purple in colour).

oyster fungus (for Catherine Gilonis, who trusted me enough to eat them after we found a batch on Wimbledon Common).

dung roundhead (for Jonathan Williams): seen in majestic profusion on a walk with Jonathan and Tom Meyer on the Howgill Fells north of Dentdale. Another 'pattern-poem'.

Pelagic, 'pertaining to the ocean or high seas', is used of birds that occupy such spaces, as here the gannet, which will fly long distances to avoid over-passing even the slenderest spit of land. The epigraph is from Homer's *Odyssey*, Book III: 'Athene / seen as a sea-eagle'. The sequence was first published in the magazine-anthology *Mad Cow* 1 (Manchester, 1994).

A set of four pieces for Michael Finnissy – one of the greatest living composers in these islands – are grouped together here: **for Michael Finnissy** itself appeared first in *Vertical Images* magazine (1994); there is a submerged allusion to his 1981 piano piece *Rushes* – cinematographic rather than botanical, as is the 1968 piano piece *Song 9* (which owes its title to a film by Stan Brakhage). The poem, which describes the 'choreography' needed to signal the presence of internal silences in the piece, appeared first in *Shrike* magazine (1995); it is reprinted in the programme for the *Michael Finnissy complete piano music* concert series given by Ian Pace (1996), the poem's dedicatee, and in Caddel & Quartermain's *Other: British and Irish Poetry Since 1970* (Hanover, NH: Wesleyan University Press, 1999). Both these poems were reprinted in Brougham, Fox & Pace, *Uncommon Ground: The Music of Michael Finnissy* (Aldershot, 1997). **Afar** and **Alongside** were published together as a broadside (Hampton Wick, Surrey: Simple Vice Books, 1996). This pair bounce off two pieces by Finnissy and the poems that lie behind them: *Afar* (1966–67), for chamber ensemble, titled from Beckett's translation of Eluard's 'A perte de vue', and *Alongside* (1979), for chamber orchestra, titled from Trakl's 'Trompeten'.

The Inscriptions was published by Ian Hamilton Finlay in his 'Echoes Series', with a facing-page 'echo' by him (*'The Inscriptions' [Echoes Series]* [Dunsyre, Lanark: Wild Hawthorn Press, 1995]). Both poems were reprinted in *Green Waters* (Stromness, Orkney: The Pier Arts Centre/Edinburgh: Polygon/Edinburgh: Morning Star/Lochmaddy, North Uist: Taigh Chearsabhagh: pocketbooks, 1998). My poem owes its origin to an Appendix in J.D. Beazley's *Attic Red-Figure Vase-Painters* (Oxford, 1963), in which Beazley says most classical Greek vase-painters were declaredly homosexual; the so-called '*kalos*-names', the names of boys who were said to be *kalos*, 'beautiful', appear in inscriptions, usually on the unseen base of the pot. These names are important tools for attribution and analysis. A handful of minor vase-painters were openly heterosexual; Beazley's Appendix IV lists their '*kale*-names': those of women once thought beautiful, of whom almost no smaller trace could be left.

Window, Light Outside started out as an attempt to map Horace's *Epistle* II.iii (known colloquially as the 'Ars Poetica') against Gustaf Sobin's 1984 long poem 'The Earth as Air: an Ars Poetica'. I cannot now trace all the quotations and allusions, but the opening echoes Horace's (re-shaping a quotation from *Richard II* via Zukofsky, a horse-obsessive); '[*man*] *reden kann*' is from Wittgenstein's *Tractatus*. Water forget-me-not is *M. scorpioides*; the 'trees' leaves' passage is after 'Ars Poetica' lines 60–61. The Greek word for 'truth', ἀλήθεια, comes from ληθώ, 'to be unknown, hidden', with α-, a 'prefix of privation'. The resultant semi-mystical reading of 'truth-as-disclosing', and the 'earthen jug', are both Heideggerian (a now thoroughly *lapsed* enthusiasm). However the jug also comes from late paintings by Georges Braque (there was a splendid exhibition at the Royal Academy in 1997), as do the lemon and other still-life items. Horace, too, praises the 'banquets of a frugal table'. Roger Tabor's *The Private Life of the Domestic Cat* provided an anatomical detail which helped explain an R.B. Kitaj drawing, *My Cat and her Husband*, which lies behind one passage. Gilbert White's wasp is described in his letter of 7 July 1797 in *The Natural History of Selborne*. 'Clarity' is as always here from George Oppen; in this instance from his poem 'Route':

> Clarity, clarity, surely clarity is the most beautiful
>   thing in the world,
> A limited, limiting clarity

The sun shines off the sea through the doorway of the cloister on the Venetian cemetery island of San Michele. The poem's title comes from a photograph by Bill Culbert, described in the poem and reproduced on the front cover of the anthology *The Invisible Reader* (London: Invisible Books, 1995), in which the poem first appeared.

Reading Hölderlin on Orkney was written up from notes made around Rackwick on the island of Hoy in March 1995; I had Richard Sieburth's remarkable edition of Hölderlin's *Hymns and Fragments* with me. Scraps of it made their way into what I wrote, indicated in the poem in **boldface**. There are snippets of Ian Hamilton Finlay's 'Orkney Lyrics', which were reprinted in the same issue of *Oar* in which these poems first appeared; Finlay stole from Engels (via Hugh MacDiarmid) before I did. A phrase comes from the anomalously Gaelic rather than Orcadian singing of Talitha MacKenzie, but I have made proper use of Hugh Marwick's magisterial *The Orkney Norn* – see therein for *geo*, a narrow coastal gully with the sea at its bottom, and *tullimentan*, 'scintillating, twinkling', the latter semi-anglicised at the close. Berriedale is a tiny cleft off the side of a deep-bottomed glacial valley on

Hoy; it is thought that glacial ice, unable to penetrate it, left pre-glacial flora able to survive there, as they do to this day. The Burn of Light is a nearby stream; it and all the other place-names are on the Ordnance Survey 1:25000 sheet for Hoy (OS 462). The sequence first appeared in *Oar* magazine from Kirkwall, Orkney (1995), and then as a stand-alone book (Hampton Wick, Surrey: gri*ll*e and Simple Vice Books, 1997), reprinted, again on Orkney (Harray: Brae Editions, 2010).

"...**both buoyed and clever...**" was collaged out of chapters 22, 23 and 24 of R.L. Stevenson's 1883 *Treasure Island* – the section of that book subtitled 'the cruise of the coracle'. It was published as a postcard as an affectionate nod to Coracle-the-publisher, very much in the spirit of Simon Cutts's own note on that pocket-sized vessel.

Pibroch (Scots Gaelic *piobaireachd*, literally 'piping') is the high-art mode of Scots bagpipe music. In a *pibroch* an initial tune or 'ground' (the *urlar*) is repeated first in reduced form (the 'thumb-variation') and then with each melody-note surrounded by an incrementally-increasing halo of grace-notes, ending in the ludicrously ornate 'crown-variation'; a performance closing with a repeat of the unadorned ground. My sequence is an attempt to rep-licate this verbally. Two sections appeared in the booklet for the *Smallest Poetry Festival in the World* (Tooting, London: Ship of Fools, 1994) and the whole as a book (Edinburgh: Morning Star Publications, 1996), with fac-ing-page Gaelic translations by Maoilios Caimbeul. The base melody of a *piobaireachd* could be a well-known tune; having seen the curious adaptation of herons to the treeless Hebridean shores, I was struck by Sorley Maclean's poem 'A' Chorra-Ghridheach' ('The Heron'), and took some features from it as my 'ground'.

walk the line records walking many miles along the length of the Chesil Beach (a long pebbly tombolo-spit on the coast of Dorset); it was first published in *OBJECT Permanence* magazine (1996) and as a book (London: Last adanA, 2000). Passages in *italics* are translated/adapted from *haiku* by Buson, Issa, Sampu and Shiki. The related poem **thinking of Evan,/walking on Chesil** is the opening of an abandoned attempt to expand the theme; it first appeared in a *Sub Voicive Poetry Programme* for a reading on 30 April 1996. 'Evan' is the saxophonist Evan Parker.

Webern sings *The Keel Row* **for Howard**, that is, as a birthday gift for the composer Howard Skempton; it first appeared in the anthology *PIECES for Howard Skempton*, published as *Spanner* issue 35, guest-edited by me

(1997). This is my one dodecaphonic poem, complete with a retrograde of its 'row' after a more traditional interlude; Skempton has written a setting of 'The Keel Row' for piano.

The **six translations of Matsuo Bashō's** *fūryū-no / hajime ya oku no / ta-ue-uta* **inside a poem for Cecilia Vicuña** are exactly that; they occupy the odd stanzas. Bashō's poem speaks of the connection between 'high' art and everyday labour, as does the work of the Chile-born sculptor, installation artist, weaver, singer and poet Cecilia Vicuña. As a piece of quasi-Oulipian play, the even stanzas – which expand on the *haiku* – draw on its Japanese vocabulary via a Spanish-English dictionary (*fūryū*, 'culture', transmutes into *fuego*, 'fire', for example). The poem appeared first in *Boxkite* magazine, and was published as a booklet that same year (London: Gri*ll*e, 1997).

* **WIND KEEN** is a reworking of an anonymous old Welsh poem, 'Y Gaeaf' ('Winter'), from the tenth/eleventh century (it is found in the 'Black Book of Carmarthen' MS); it opens with four four-lettered words, *llym awel llwm bryn*, which fall naturally into English likewise: 'Keen gust bare hill'. Remembering Hamish Fulton's artwork recording a walk in Canada's Baffin Island, *ROCK / FALL / ECHO / DUST*, I wondered if it would be possible to replicate the world of 'Y Gaeaf' in a similar manner.

an egg for E. appeared first in *Oyster Boy Review* (1999); an inedible Easter-Egg, after the fashion of the ancient Greek pattern-poet Simias.

remembering Scott LaFaro also first appeared in *Oyster Boy Review* (1999); LaFaro is the great jazz bassist (Ornette Coleman, Bill Evans…) who died young in a car-crash.

* **Wedding-Song** was written for my musician friends Richard and Mary. The **boldface** elements derive from the *epithalamia* of Sappho and Catullus.

The **century's end** *ghazal* was written on 31 December 2000, some way after Thomas Hardy's 'The Darkling Thrush' (dated 31 December 1900); it was published as an end-of-year/century/millennium card. The implicit 'signature' of the *ghazal* is that of the (un-named) thrush.

* **a small** *alba* comes from the notebook for a visit to a private garden in Provence, filled with work by Ian Hamilton Finlay. An *alba* is a Provençal dawn-song (as against the northern *aubade*); the shape of this one has something in common with some works by Finlay.

* **pond…** is another notebook poem; it collates some English translations of the opening of Bashō's famous *haiku, furuike ya*.

* The **Afghan *ghazal*** is a response to Tony Baker and Richard Caddel's collaborative *Monksnailsongs* (Bray, Co. Wicklow, Éire: Wild Honey Press, 2002); it draws on Blanford and Godwin-Austen, *Fauna of British India: Mollusca…* (1908) and Simms, *In Afghanistan* (2001), and makes passing use of the titles of Ernst Bloch's *Das Prinzip Hoffnung* and Günter Grass's *From the Diary of a Snail*. This *ghazal* is collectively 'signed' by the molluscs who inhabit it.

The **sound shanty for bob cobbing** first appeared in *for Bob Cobbing: a celebration* (Sutton, Surrey: Mainstream Poetry, 2000). It lists Scottish islands uninhabited as of 1974. There are doubtless more now.

The 2001 **Three Misreadings of Horatian Odes** first appeared in *Quid* 9, the 'Against Imperialism' issue (2002). They recognise that whilst the poet Horace (who had fought for the Roman republic in the field against Octavian/ Augustus) had good pragmatic reasons *personally* for writing poems urging that Emperor to attack Arabia, the poems themselves remain inexcusable. As do the actions of those who excused like imbecilities two millennia later. The 'misreadings' are, in order, those of liberal cultural commentators, western statesmen, and the author; the last-listed needs to apologise for using elements from the unimpeachable commentaries of Nisbet & Hubbard in these 'odes'.

* Another Gulf War piece, **foreign policy**, uses search-and-replace software on a core text. It has been performed with live improvised musical accompaniment and/or electronic treatment in the UK and at an arts festival in Sweden.

white came about the day I went to see a small exhibition of small and (mostly) white paintings by Robert Ryman, all of which had single-word titles (I think in the Mayor Gallery in the early '80s?). I was taken by the array of technical possibilities the paintings displayed – different densities of paint, speed and precision of application, even the relationship with the frames; and found myself considering the one-word titles as sorts of 'frames' as well. The methodology was to use *Roget's Thesaurus* to match synonyms for 'white' and for the title-words. In theory it need never stop… It was published in *The Other Room Anthology* 6 (Manchester: The Other Room Press, 2014).

Taliesin was first published online among Peter Quartermain's edited tributes to the poet Richard Caddel, in *Jacket* 20 (http://jacketmagazine.com/20/quart-cadd.htm), 2003. It makes some use of one of his favoured techniques – 'loose phonic translation' – used on a poem from one of his (and my) favourite literatures, early Welsh poetry; here a poem from the *Canu Taliesin* beginning 'Kynan kat diffret…', chosen because it mentions, as I thus do, a once-famous Welsh ruling family, the Cadelling, descendants of a 'Cadell'.

for Louis Zukofsky, a hundred years on was first published as a postcard by Coracle, Ballybeg, Éire, in 2004 – the centenary of Zukofsky's birth, which went pretty much as unmarked as the anniversaries of his death have (save for the anthology I edited ten years after his death – see note to 'Daruma' above). This poem makes use of the text surrounding the line from *Two Gentlemen of Verona* that Zukofsky used for his dark 'valentine' for Cid Corman, 'Julia's Wild', incorporated into his long and astonishing Shakespearian meditation *Bottom: on Shakespeare*.

The germ of the ***unHealed*** project was re-reading the fragmentary old Welsh poem-cycle the *Canu Heledd* ('Songs of Heledd'). I was reading a line, *Eglwysseu Bassa collasant eu breint* ('The churches at Bassa have lost their privileges/status'), when, as I looked, the churches at Bassa became the houses at Basra in Iraq, and *collasant* became 'collapsed', *breint* 'burnt'. And that was that; the impetus was imperative, to take a relatively unknown, once everyday tale of English soldiery invading a neighbouring country and behaving badly – and bring it up-to-date. In part I did this and produced reasonably accurate translations (as the first, and especially the second, group of stanzas); but also unreasonably inaccurate ones – as e.g. using a Chinese-English dictionary. Iraqi place-names replace similar-sounding Welsh ones throughout, for obvious reasons. The *dinar* is an Iraqi coin; the *oud* a Middle-Eastern stringed instrument, ancestor of the lute; a *co-ax* is British army slang for a weapon mounted 'co-axially' to work in unison with another larger or smaller one, as (e.g.) a machine-gun aligned with the main gun on a tank; *hesh* stands for 'high-explosive squash head', a type of ammunition particularly effective against tank armour – and buildings. The sections included here use, amongst other techniques, relatively straight translation (stanza groups 1 and 2, the former with more of the modern world); phonetically-derived substitution from external texts (ornithological material in stanza group 3, interrupting a more focussed reading non-logically; an 'Open Letter to the Iraqi People' by Tony Blair in stanza group 7, ending in the original Welsh phrase; and reports of the cruise-missile attack on Shu'ale marketplace in stanza group 9); vocabulary generated phonetically from the original Welsh (stanza groups 4, 5 and 6, with differing degrees of reworking). The two list-poems (stanza groups 8 and 11) name 'rulers' of the region, and names assigned to' oil-fields therein (though, of course, the war was never about oil). The penultimate section (stanza group 10) draws on arms-dealer promo. prose, plus that company's 'ethics policy'. I couldn't make it up. [Stanza groups 1 and 2 appeared in *Angel Exhaust* magazine (2006); stanza group 4 in *The New Review of Literature* (2006); stanza groups 5 and 8 in the magazine *Poetry Wales* (2008), reprinted in Goodby and Davies, *The Edge of Necessary: Welsh Innovative Poetry 1966– 2016* (Llangattock, Powys: Aquifer Books, in association with Boiled String Press, Swansea, 2018); stanza group 6 appeared on the website *Archive of the Now* (www.archiveofthenow.org), uploaded 2006; stanza groups 7, 9, 10 and 11 in *…further evidence of nerves: Cambridge Poetry Summit 2005* (Cambridge: Barque/Arehouse, 2005) and in *Readings: Small Publishers Fair 2004* (Research Group for Artists' Publications, Cromford, Derbys, 2005). * Stanza group 3 was rewritten for this book, and is thus previously unpublished.]

Processions written inside chivalry first appeared in *Issue 1* online (2008). It is accurately signed on the page, as the 'poem' wasn't 'written' by 'me', or indeed by anyone; its text appeared as part of a vast corpus of well over a thousand pages, assembled by a web-surfing 'bot' which turned text-extracts into poem-like entities and randomly ascribed them under the names of poets with a digital presence. Some 'victims' of this process tried to locate and take legal proceedings against the responsible parties. I take a broader view of authorship, and am happy to acknowledge my nominal responsibility here; indeed, I have sought out (and been granted) formal permission by the editor of *Issue 1* to reprint 'my' 'poem' here. *Issue 1* itself is no longer online, but a cloned version survives at www.stephenmclaughlin.net/issue-1/ Issue-1_Fall-2008.pdf; you will find many, many poems therein that are equally *not* by their authors (John Ashbery, Thomas A Clark, Hadewijch of Antwerp, Vanessa Place, William Shakespeare, Robert Sheppard…).

* **Blair's Grave** is the title often given to Robert Blair's once well-known poem of 1743, *The Grave*. William Blake made in 1805 a series of illustrations for it, and wrote a connected poem, 'Dedication of the Illustrations to Blair's *Grave*'. My sequence makes use of this material, together with speeches by Tony Blair and remarks made on a range of political blogs at the time of his resignation. These poems make *selective* use of material generated by an online cut-up engine, making a contrast to the wholly *mechanical* construction of the preceding piece.

NORTH HILLS is my collective title for a very large group of 'faithless' translations from old Chinese originals. I've discussed its methodology in the front-matter to two books drawn from that corpus (*eye-blink* and '*North Hills*') and the interested reader is directed thence. In short, my contention is that the *syntactic* practice of some Chinese writing is of considerable poetic interest. Chinese characters are *in themselves* immutable; such modification as they receive is achieved by the addition of other words/characters acting as articles or personal pronouns; these are often dispensed with in poetry. This omission opens up an indeterminate space for the reader to enter and play. Such poems, common in the T'ang dynasty in particular, avoid restricting action to a specific agent (or even gendering that agent) and also refrain from committing such action to one specific time. Obviously it is impossible to replicate such effects, which rely on specificities of literary Chinese, in English; so the *NORTH HILLS* poems set out to do just that. For this reason all the poems gathered here are given in more than one version, in a direct attempt to show the implicit variety held in their originals. They loop round alphabetically to start and end with versions of a poem often said to be the most impermeably difficult in all Chinese literature...

The first Li Shang-yin text was made as a unique poem-card for an improvised performance of Chris Goode & Jonny Liron's *World of Work* (Sussex Poetry Festival, Brighton, 2010), with each Chinese character represented by a single English word; it was reprinted online at Infinite Editions (www.infiniteeditions.blogspot.co.uk); second version *. Li's original refers *en passant* to the famous philosopher dreaming he is a butterfly, or vice versa, paradox.

The second Po Chü-I version was published in *eye-blink* (London: Veer Books, 2010); the first version *. 'Flamingo feathers' is a form of the decorative plant *Celosia argentea*. The second version is dedicated to the poet Jeff Hilson, author of *A grasses primer* (London: Form Books, 2000); 'timothy' is an actual grass (*Phleum pratense*).

The twin versions of Tai Shu-lun were made for an anthology celebrating the joint sixtieth birthdays of the poets Alan Halsey and Gavin Selerie, *Salamanders & Mandrake: Gavin Selerie & Alan Halsey at Sixty* (Wakefield: ISPress, 2009). There are borrowings from their work.

The first T'ao Ch'ien version appeared in *veer off* magazine (2008), and is dedicated to Sean Bonney; second version *. Galtymore is an Irish mountain; Simon Cutts's reworking of a line of Mallarmé is here reworked, after a photo he took in his seventieth birthday year; the poem is for him.

The Chinese original of Ts'ui Hao's poem alludes to the anonymous 'Summoning the Recluse' (from the second-century AD anthology *Ch'u Tz'u* ['Songs of the South']); I've used a line from Wordsworth's 'The Recluse' in its stead (in the first version only). The second version nods amicably to Bill Griffiths's 'Version of Ts'ui Hao's Poem of the

Pavilion of a Taoist Sage', and was done in thanks to Alan Halsey and Ken Edwards for their work in editing Griffiths's *Collected Earlier Poems*. (Both versions *.)

Both Ts'ui Shu versions are *; the second borrows a phrase from Couvreur's French translation of the Chinese 'Classic of History' (*Shu Ching*) which drifted into my head many years after first meeting Ezra Pound quoting it in one of the Cantos in *Rock-Drill*. Not literary reference but live memory.

The first Tu Fu version appeared in *Damn the Cæsars* magazine (2008), and is dedicated to Karen Brookman; it was read at one of her salons; second version *.

The first Tu Mu version appeared in the erroneously titled '*North Hills*', which appeared as an issue of *Free Poetry* magazine (2009) – the correct title should have been *Minor Players*; second version *.

'Tzü Yeh', a nominally female poet, is almost certainly fictitious, though not my invention. Both versions of 'her' poem *.

The first Wang Wei version (of what is arguably the most famous Chinese poem) appeared in *Wheel River* (London: Contraband, 2015), featuring the entirety of a co-written sequence by Wang and his friend P'ei Ti. An enlarged reprint will include a further seven translations of this poem in an appendix (though *not* the second version here, made for this book *).

Wei Shuang's poem is set in the 'Jinling landscape' that features in J.H. Prynne's *Kazoo Dreamboats*, and the second version here uses only vocabulary from that book. The first version echoes a photograph by its dedicatee, Fern Bryant, seen in an exhibition of photos of China. (Both versions *.)

The poem by Yü Hsuan-chi (with 'Tzü Yeh' the only female poet herein) was commissioned for 'A certain slant of light: in response to the work of Emily Dickinson', held under the aegis of the London-based events series POLYply; the second version uses only Dickinson's vocabulary to translate the same poem. (Both versions *.)

Both Ch'ien Ch'i versions *; the second one is for David Rees.

The first Li Po version appeared in *Veer Away* magazine (2007) and *Damn the Cæsars* magazine (2008), and was reprinted in *eye-blink* (London: Veer Books, 2010); the second version was made for this book *. The poem uses a recurring Chinese poetic trope, visiting a sage in a remote retreat and finding him away. Li concentrates in consequence on what 'is' 'there', the landscape.

The penultimate Li Shang-yin version appeared in *eye-blink* (London: Veer Books, 2010); the final version was written as a sixtieth-birthday gift for Robert Sheppard, and recognises some of his vocabulary and enthusiasms (e.g. blues harmonica, or 'mouth-harp'). 'The cuckoo is a pretty bird, she warbles as she flies' is an Appalachian folk-song, of British origin, collected by Harry Smith. This final Li Shang-yin poem appeared in *An Educated Desire: Robert Sheppard at 60*, ed. Scott Thurston (Newton-le-Willows: Knives Forks and Spoons Press, 2015).

* **an epithalamy, or ballad** was written for the wedding of my artist and curator friends David and Carolyn, at Harty (on the Isle of Sheppey off the north Kent coast), a potential site for the hall of Heorot – which explains why stanza 2 combines *Beowulf*'s lines 8 (*under wolcnum*), 93 (*swá wæter bebúgeð*) and 211 (*under beorge*). The Latin tag – 'as the clinging ivy / embraces the tree' – is from Catullus, poem LXI, an epithalamium; 'unconcealment' is Greek ἀ-λήθεια (again! – here reflecting David's interest in Heidegger) and 'rest and peace' come, as they would, from Bach (specifically the Cantata BWV 208: 'Kann man Ruh und Friede spüren'). The title comes from George Puttenham's 1589 *Arte of English Poesie*; as with the other wedding-poem collected here, use is made of Sappho (and Catullus) as also Spenser.

* **Bass adds Bass** was written for the bass player Dominic Lash and performed at his 'farewell' concert/leaving party in London's Café OTO before a temporary move to New York in early 2011. The title and a few words are lifted from the very fine song *Bass Adds Bass* by Family Fodder. The party performance by myself with Dom Lash on bass was filmed by Helen Petts: www.youtube.com/watch?v=1PmFR5xNhjE

Georg Trakl fails to write a Christmas poem – the nearest he got, according to a title index I started from, were 'Im Winter', 'Wintergang in a-Moll' and 'Winternacht'. Phrases from these are permuted, a notion I got after prolonged contemplation of his often exceedingly eccentric usage of colour-words. This was published as a year's-end card in 2014.

David Davis's bone density was written for *Badge of Shame*, one of a series of responsive anthologies, *Purges* (edited anonymously and with no place of publication given, but declared to be a 'strong and stable production', 2017). It was prompted by the widely reported suggestion of the elder statesman it commemorates, that refugee children should have their teeth x-rayed to assess their age – and thus whether their plight should count for anything. Since the poem was written and first published Davis has, of course, been promoted to glory, and his density has become common knowledge worldwide. There is a snatch of dentally related speech from the film *Marathon Man* near the close.

* **The Matter of Ireland** is a term for the corpus of mediaeval Welsh stories involving Ireland (e.g. 'Branwen, daughter of Llyr' in the *Mabinogion*). Here, again, 'matter' is taken literally, applying a simple acrostic process to the title of a book (London: Writers Forum, 1996) by the dedicatee, the Irish poet Billy Mills (co-publisher with Catherine Walsh of my first book). I have re-used minerals named in Billy's book, without checking that they are in fact found in Ireland; that correlation was more important than strict geological accuracy.

Revisions (after Roy Fisher) was published online in *Molly Bloom* (http://mollybloom-tributes.weebly.com), in a memorial supplement for the late Roy Fisher (2017). The poem wrote itself, many years ago now, onto a scrap of paper that ended up interleaved in a book of Roy's poems; it is a *Widerruf*, or poetic reversal, of the fifth of his 1980s set of 'New Diversions':

> *Vigil*
> *taking over hours and losing them*
> *into a moist gleam,*
> *a single light*

The Latin tag translates roughly as 'that activity might through reflection forge the various arts' (*Georgics* 1.133); Fisher was of course a highly adept jazz pianist as well as a great poet.

Coping Batter (for Tom Raworth) was published online in *Molly Bloom* (http://mollybloom-tributes.weebly.com), in a memorial supplement for the late and much-missed Tom Raworth (2017).

a breath of air was commissioned to accompany the CD release of a 2008 concert of solo soprano saxophone improvisations by Evan Parker (*whitstable solo*, Psi 10.01). Parker has run through this book subliminally as well as openly: he's said that *piobaireachd* is influential on his work, and he recorded with Steve Lacy. This poem takes its intricate stanza-structure and rhyme-scheme from 'l'aura amara…' by the twelfth-century troubadour Arnaut Daniel, in an attempt to hint at the complexity of Parker's playing. That untranslatable word for pure pleasure, *jouissance*, is from Barthes; a *chalumeau* is a pastoral (thus 'unsophisticated') reed instrument; the fourth stanza in part describes the interior of St Peter's church, Whitstable, where the solos were recorded; *gemutató* ('presentation') was cited by Parker from Bartók on a previous solo recording; *de motu* is the Latin title of a piece of writing by Parker, available online (www.efi.group.shef.ac.uk/fulltext/demotu.html); *remir* is the Occitan word for 'I gaze', found in the corresponding line in Arnaut's original (a different poem, though, than the one Pound remembers as the focus of a moment of *jouissance* in Canto XX). The poem was written for Evan Parker's CD, but would like to remember the late Bill Griffiths, one of the few poets writing in English who could rival Arnaut Daniel for complexity and breadth of in-ventiveness.

ACKNOWLEDGEMENTS

I owe my principal debt of thanks to Tony Baker and the late Richard Caddel, my first friends in the world of poetry (and outside it, too, impor-tantly); and to Billy Mills and Catherine Walsh, who offered me the chance of book-publication at a point when I was about to turn my energies to other things. More recently I am indebted to Peter Manson, who nagged at me for years to consider the notion of a Selected Poems (and later was of direct practical assistance); and in the recent past to Luke Allan, for acting, independently, on Peter's suggestion; and finally to Elizabeth James, for ster-ling, sometimes stern, advice, and much hard graft helping me get this book into shape.

I have been at some pains to give as full an account as I could of my small participation in the wide web of small presses and little magazines that throughout the 1980s and on were of immense importance in supporting a wide range of writers and writing over a long period of time when outlets of more notional consequence took little or no interest. For prior publication (or major involvement therein) thanks are due to David Aldridge; David Annwn (in his own right and with Frances Presley and Peterjon & Yasmin Skelt); David Ashford; Tim Atkins; Kevin Bailey; Tony Baker; Jeffery Beam; Andrea Brady; Henrietta Brougham, Christopher Fox & Ian Pace; Rodger Brown; the late Richard Caddel (in his own right and with Ann Caddel and with Peter Quartermain); Maoilios Caimbeul; Maxine Chernoff & Paul Hoover; Adrian Clarke & Lawrence Upton; Bob Cobbing; David Connearn; Martin Corless-Smith; Sara Crangle & Sam Ladkin; Bill Culbert; Simon Cutts & Erica Van Horn; Andrew Duncan (with Tim Allen, and with Charles Bainbridge); Alec Finlay; the late Ian Hamilton Finlay; Allen Fisher; John Goodby & Lyndon Davies; Terrel Hale; Robert Hampson; Tom Jenks & James Davies; Andrew Lawson & Anthony Mellors; Rupert Loydell; Steve McLaughlin & Jim Carpenter (reproduced by kind permission); Peter Manson; Roy Miki; Billy Mills & Catherine Walsh; Peter Mortimer; Alec Newman & Scott Thurston; Rich Owens; Ian Pace; Andrew Parkinson, Duncan McLean & Alistair Peebles; the late Evangeline Paterson; Alistair Peebles (in his own right); Bridget Penney & Paul Holman; Helen Petts; Robin Purves & Peter Manson; Peter Quartermain (in his own right, and with the late Richard Caddel, and with John Tranter); David Rees (in his own right, and with Simon Smith); the late Ian Robinson; Aidan Semmens; Robert Sheppard & Patricia Farrell; Zoë Skoulding; Simon Smith (in his own right, and with David Rees); the late Geoffrey Soar; Andrew Spragg; Colin Still; Keston Sutherland; James Taylor; Scott Thurston; John Tranter & Peter Quartermain; Lawrence Upton; Erica Van Horn (in her own right, and with Simon Cutts); Paul Vangelisti; the Veer Books collective (William Rowe, Ulli Freer, Stephen Mooney, Aodán McCardle, Piers Hugill, Adrian Clarke, Carol Watts); Jont Whittington; Paul Wright & Jo Marriner; Luke Youngman; Yt Communications (Frances Kruk & Sean Bonney), and the anonymous editor of *Badge of Shame*. Also, for their artwork in and on the book, David Connearn (photography: Andrew Penketh) and David Rees; and for last-minute assistance and technical overviews, Neil Crawford, Simon McFadden and Ken Macpherson. Thanks to all.